普通高等院校"十四五"规划旅游管理专业类精品教材
国家级一流本科专业建设旅游管理专业特色教材

# 旅游专业英语
## Tourism English

主　编　韦夏婵

华中科技大学出版社
http://press.hust.edu.cn
中国·武汉

# 内 容 简 介

本书分为三大模块,第一模块为专业基础理论阅读,介绍本单元主题的基础理论,要求学生掌握相关专业术语,能描述和讨论相关旅游现象;第二模块为情景对话,主要训练学生在旅游业一线岗位谈论相关主题的交际能力;第三模块为中国故事,要求学生系统了解中国概况、传统文化和现代化建设成就,具备在涉外活动中传播中国文化的能力。同时教师还可鼓励学有余力的学生对拓展阅读中的词条进一步挖掘,提高他们探究现象、表达观点的能力。

**图书在版编目(CIP)数据**

旅游专业英语/韦夏婵主编.—武汉:华中科技大学出版社,2021.7(2024.8重印)
ISBN 978-7-5680-7341-7

Ⅰ.①旅… Ⅱ.①韦… Ⅲ.①旅游-英语-高等学校-教材 Ⅳ.①F59

中国版本图书馆 CIP 数据核字(2021)第 141328 号

**旅游专业英语**　　　　　　　　　　　　　　　　　　　韦夏婵　主编
Lüyou Zhuanye Yingyu

策划编辑:王　乾
责任编辑:陈　然
封面设计:原色设计
责任校对:阮　敏
责任监印:周治超
出版发行:华中科技大学出版社(中国·武汉)　　电话:(027)81321913
　　　　　武汉市东湖新技术开发区华工科技园　　邮编:430223
录　　排:华中科技大学惠友文印中心
印　　刷:武汉科源印刷设计有限公司
开　　本:787mm×1092mm　1/16
印　　张:11.25
字　　数:340千字
版　　次:2024 年 8 月第 1 版第 3 次印刷
定　　价:50.00 元

本书若有印装质量问题,请向出版社营销中心调换
全国免费服务热线:400-6679-118　竭诚为您服务
版权所有　侵权必究

普通高等学校"十四五"规划旅游管理类精品教材
国家级一流本科专业建设旅游管理类特色教材

# 出版说明

为深入落实全国教育大会和《加快推进教育现代化实施方案(2018—2022年)》文件精神,贯彻落实新时代全国高校本科教育工作会议和《教育部关于加快建设高水平本科教育全面提高人才培养能力的意见》、"六卓越一拔尖"计划2.0系列文件要求,推动新工科、新医科、新农科、新文科建设,做强一流本科、建设一流专业、培养一流人才,全面振兴本科教育,提高高校人才培养能力,实现高等教育内涵式发展,教育部决定全面实施"六卓越一拔尖"计划2.0,启动一流本科专业建设"双万计划",并计划在2019—2021年,建设143个旅游管理类国家级一流本科专业点。

基于此,建设符合旅游管理类国家级一流本科专业人才培养需求的教材,将助力旅游高等教育专业结构优化,全面打造一流本科人才培养体系,进而为中国旅游业在"十四五"期间深化文旅融合、持续迈向高质量发展提供有力支撑。

华中科技大学出版社一向以服务高校教学、科研为己任,重视高品质专业教材出版,"十三五"期间,在教育部高等学校旅游管理类专业教学指导委员会和全国高校旅游应用型本科院校联盟的大力支持和指导下,率先组织编纂出版"普通高等院校旅游管理专业类'十三五'规划精品教材"。该套系教材自出版发行以来,被全国三百多所开设旅游管理类专业的院校选用,并多次再版。

为积极响应"十四五"期间国家一流本科专业建设的新需求,"国家级一流本科专业建设旅游管理专业特色教材"项目应运而生。本项目依据旅游管理类国家级一流本科专业建设要求,立足"十四五"期间旅游管理人才培养新特征进行整体规划,邀请旅游管理类国家级一流本科专业建设院校国家教学名师、资深教授及中青年旅游学科带头人加盟编纂。

该套教材融入思政内容,助力旅游管理教学实现立德树人与专业人才培养有机融合。让学生充分认识专业学习的重要性,注意学生专业知识技能的培养,并将学生个人职业发展与国家建设紧密结合,使其树立正确的价值观。同时,本套教材基于旅游管理类国家级一流本科专业建设要求,在教材内容上体现"两性一度",即创新性和高阶性、挑战度的高质量要求。此外，依托资源服务平台，打造新形态立体教材。华中科技大学出版社紧抓"互联网＋"时代教育需求，自主研发并上线了华中出版资源服务平台为本套系教材提供立体化教学配套服务，既为教师教学提供便捷，提供教学计划书、教学课件、习题库、案例库、参考答案、教学视频等系列配套教学资源，又为教学管理提供便捷，构建课程开发、习题管理、学生评论、班级管理等于一体的教学生态链，打造出线上线下、课内课外的新形态立体化互动教材。

　　本项目编委会力求通过出版一套兼具理论与实践、传承与创新、基础与前沿的精品教材，为我国加快实现旅游高等教育内涵式发展、建成世界旅游强国贡献一份力量，并诚挚邀请更多致力于中国旅游高等教育的专家学者加入我们！

党的二十大报告指出,"高质量发展是全面建设社会主义现代化国家的首要任务"以党的二十大精神为指引,推进文化自信自强,推动文化旅游业高质量发展,是全面建设社会主义现代化国家的重要举措之一。文旅产业的高质量发展对文旅从业人员的素质提出了更高的要求。旅游专业本科学生不仅需要具备良好的语言交际能力,表达观点、解决问题的能力,还需要注重文化底蕴、人文情怀、价值理念和社会服务意识的培养。

本书以旅游过程涉及的各个产业为主题,不仅训练学生在工作岗位上的英语交际能力,而且拓展学生在旅游行业的可持续发展能力,使其具备在工作和社交过程中传播中国文化的能力。本教材具有以下特点:

(1) 专业理论够用为度。专业英语是外语教学与专业知识的结合,旅游管理本科专业英语教学应区别于高职高专以"工作过程"为导向的一线服务情景对话。本书每一单元都辅以旅游专业基础理论阅读,要求学生能够掌握旅游业基础理论的专业术语,能够描述并讨论旅游业相关现象。

(2) 体现旅游行业发展新态势。科技的进步带来旅游业态的多样化、形式与内容的多元化。本教材在对话、阅读中选用最新数据,结合近年来旅游行业发展新态势,力求拓宽学生视野,实现在校学习与行业发展的无缝连接。

(3) 培养学生的"文化自信"。本教材设置的"中国故事"模块不仅系统地介绍了中国概况,还介绍了中国改革开放建设所取得的成就,不仅能增强学生的文化自信,也有助于他们在涉外活动中更好地传播中国文化。

(4) 用合作探究学习培养思辨能力。改变以知识呈现为主的填空、翻译等练习形式,以讨论、分析、总结、分享旅游业相关主题的方式培养学生的合作探究学习能力,注重培养学生的思辨能力和跨文化交际能力。每个单元的拓展阅读以词条的形式补充了大量素材,希望在加大语言材料输入的基础上,培养学生探究现象、表达观点的能力。

由于时间仓促,编者水平有限,教材中难免存在疏漏之处,恳请各位同仁和老师、同学们在使用过程中批评指正。

编者<br/>2021 年 4 月

# 目录
Contents

| Unit 1 | Introduction to Tourism | /1 |
| Unit 2 | Tourist Transportation | /17 |
| Unit 3 | Travel Agency | /32 |
| Unit 4 | Hotel Accommodation | /48 |
| Unit 5 | Food and Beverage Service | /65 |
| Unit 6 | Tourist Destination | /85 |
| Unit 7 | Tourist Attraction | /103 |
| Unit 8 | Recreation and Entertainment | /119 |
| Unit 9 | Tourist Shopping | /136 |
| Unit 10 | New Trends of Tourism | /152 |

参考文献　　　　　　　　　　　　　　　　　　　　　　/167

# Unit 1
# Introduction to Tourism

**Learning Objectives**

After learning this part, you should be able to:
1. describe the nature of tourism activities, define tourism and tourist.
2. discuss the benefits of tourism industry.
3. describe the development of Chinese tourism industry.
4. develop your patriotism by learning how to deliver a general introduction of China.

## Lead In

Classify the following workplaces into corresponding departments.

| tour guide | waiter | hostess | tour leader | tour operator |
| bellman | waitress | housekeeper | receptionist | chef |
| concierge | therapist | butler | sommelier | shop assistant |
| driver | barista | baker | interpreter | travel consultant |
| bartender | coach | pilot | flight attendant | |

| | |
|---|---|
| Transportation | |
| Accommodation | |
| Food & Beverage | |
| Sightseeing | |

| Shopping | |
| --- | --- |
| Recreation | |

## Background Reading

### Tourism Industry

Tourism is a composite of activities, services, and industries that deliver a travel experience including transportation, accommodations, eating and drinking establishments, shops, entertainment, activity facilities, and other hospitality services available for individuals or groups that are traveling away from home. According to WTO's (World Tourism Organization) definition in 1993, tourism comprises the activities of persons traveling to and staying in places outside their usual environment for not more than one year for leisure, business and other purposes.

A tourist is a person traveling to another location, away from their usual social environment, for business, pleasure or social reasons. By most accepted definitions, to be classed as a tourist, a person needs to stay at that location for more than 24 hours, but for not more than one year. Tourists may be motivated to travel by a range of different factors, such as refreshment of body and mind, or the pursuit of excitement, entertainment or pleasure. Alternatively, travelers may be driven by cultural curiosity, self-improvement, business, or by a desire to visit friends and family, or to form new relationships. While business travelers are usually classed as tourists, it is worth noting that many definitions of the word "tourist" exclude those who travel with the intention of making an income in the place that they travel to.

Travel as an aspect of human activity has a pedigree going back to thousands of years. Early travelers who were not on the road for religious reasons were usually on military, diplomatic, or political missions. In ancient Persia, traveling was done in large caravans. The idea of travel for leisure, educational or healthy purposes really came to prominence during **"Age of Enlightenment"** in the eighteenth century with the development of **"The Grand Tour"** in Europe. Paris, Rome, Florence, Venice, Munich, Vienna, and other cities of central Europe were fashionable tour stops, and resorts and spas were developed to accommodate the tourists. The costs of such travel prohibited these trips to all but the wealthy people, and it was not until the coming of the railway in the nineteenth century that opportunities were opened up for the general population. In July 1841, a British traveling salesman, Thomas Cook hired a train to send about 570 persons to participate in a party. The entire distance is approximately 22 miles. It provided free lunches with sausage and snacks for the tourists. This tour is regarded as the beginning of early modern tourism.

Industrialization has created a large number of people with an amount of **disposable income**—income above and beyond what is needed for basic expenses such as food, shelter, clothing and taxes. The emergence of **paid leave**, increased **leisure time**, the development of railway networks and air transport, most notably the jet engine, contributed to an increased number of holidays. The development of air transport and charter flights have popularized long-haul destinations. Most vacations were constructed as recreational experiences, mainly at summer and winter leisure resorts.

It was not until the 1960s that **mass tourism** began to develop in the economically developed countries, and later became popular in the world. Mass tourism is a phenomenon of large-scale packaging of standardized leisure services at fixed prices for sale to a mass clientele. The main feature of the mass tourism is standardization. It provides a **package tour** that covers transportation, accommodation, guides, food and other goods and services. The travel is pre paid, based on a strict time schedule, and the price is affordable because of the cheaper cost created through large customer volumes.

The expansion of air transport, the implementation of computer reservation systems and online bookings have largely changed the overall concept of mass tourism, resulting in new products and activities for tourist consumption. Driven by a relatively strong global economy, a growing middle class in emerging economies, technological advances, new business models, affordable travel costs and visa facilitation, international tourist arrivals grew 4% in 2019 to reach the 1.5 billion mark. This represents the tenth consecutive year of growth.

Nowadays, the tourism industry has been the fastest growing industry and the world's largest industry. By 2030, UNWTO (The United Nations World Tourism Organization) forecasts that international tourist arrivals will reach 1.8 billion.

##  ‖ Situational Dialogue

> Dialogue 1

### World Traveler

Scene: Helen (A) is a student majoring in tourism. She is talking with Jack (B), a friend who travels very often.

A: Hey, Jack, I've heard you are quite a world traveler.

B: Yeah, I love traveling. I've been to around 20 different countries. I've lived in

Cambodia, Japan and South Africa, and many different parts of the United States.

A: Do you prefer to travel with somebody or to travel alone?

B: I prefer to travel with someone, but I also enjoy being by myself.

A: When you are travling, do you like to follow a guide book or to explore and just do things without any planning?

B: I tend to be on a time budget so I do use guide books, and in general it will be the *Lonely Planet*, the same as everyone else does.

A: What do you think of backpackers?

B: I was a backpacker when I was a student. I went to lots of places in Japan, like Tokyo, Kyoto. I saved as much money as possible and hired a very cheap hotel to stay for some nights. I like the feeling to be myself, not depend on others.

A: I think backpackers are pretty cool. They want to travel around to taste life and to challenge themselves.

B: Yes, backpackers are very adventurous! You probably get to see things that you don't normally see in the regular tourist tours. So I think it's good to be a backpacker.

A: I've never actually done backpacking myself, but that is how I would travel myself because it's the cheapest way. Do you still travel as a backpacker now?

B: After work, I don't have such a long vacation, so I prefer to have a self-drive tour every year. Some regions like the southwest of the United States don't have air travel to the remote deserts, so your only option is to drive.

A: A road trip is always my dream. Driving will allow you to see everything, and you can stop at some of the smaller, more personal destination along the way.

B: Exactly! I can spend more time interacting with the local people than traditional sightseeing tour.

A: What is your favorite place in China?

B: It's difficult to answer. Err… I liked Xinjiang.

A: Xinjiang is also my dream destination. I hope that I can drive around Xinjiang in the near future.

B: You can read my blog for some tips.

A: Great! I will ask for your advice when my dream comes true.

## ▶ Dialogue 2

### Impacts of Tourism Industry

Scene: Wang Lei (A) is a student of Guilin Tourism University. He is talking with a foreign student Rick (B) from Indonesia.

A: Hello, Rick, you are from Indonesia, right? I heard that Bali Island is a beautiful paradise. Have you ever been there before?

B: So many times. When I was a child, my parents took me there to visit the gorgeous beaches in Bali Island.

A: Are there any places interesting in Bali Island?

B: Bali Island has a peaceful lifestyle, very connected to nature. Most of the people in Bali Island are Hindus. So there is a lot of Hindu temples in Bali Island. Bali Island also has very famous scenery inside like the rice fields. But I haven't been there for a long time since it is more and more expensive for us to travel to Bali Island.

A: That's weird. I had the idea that Bali Island is a part of Indonesia, so a lot of Indonesians would go there.

B: Bali Island attracts so many international tourists every year, hotels, food and travel expenses are too expensive for local people to afford.

A: Is it possible that the government try to lower down the price that local people can afford to appreciate their own beauty in Bali Island.

B: Thousands of tourists go there everywhere and the island cannot afford to hold so many tourists every day. If prices are really low, then more and more people will go there, there might be environmental problems.

A: I guess that makes sense. Developing tourism is a good way to develop local economy, especially the rural regions, but it will also cause inflation of essentials like food, clothing and housing.

B: That is true. Tourism creates jobs and opportunities for local people, but also causes problems like environmental pollution and threats to natural resources.

A: Bali Island is such an international destination. What is the attitude of the local people towards tourists? Do they welcome them or sometimes they wish these international tourists got off their island?

B: I think some of the local people do feel that way towards foreigners. They feel like they're taking over the island, that is a stereotype. But Bali Island would not survive without tourism right now, because it's our bread and butter. At the same time, tourism is bringing our culture back. People are practicing more dances, cultural traditions because tourists want to see that.

A: It is good to see that people benefit from the development of tourism. I hope something should be done by your government and you can afford to visit Bali Island in the future.

B: Hopefully something will change.

## ➢ Dialogue 3

### Planning a Tour

Scene: Sam (A) and Jane (B) are friends. They are talking about planning a tour.

A: Wow! Jane, you're going to Tibet?

B: Yes, I really need to leave this town for a change. Working day after day has worn me out. My brother and I just finished making our itinerary.

A: That's really cool! I've always dreamed of going somewhere like Tibet, seeing something unique.

B: Great minds think alike. Why don't you join us? We are leaving next week. You'll still have a week to prepare.

A: Oh, Tibet sounds great. I have a one-month vacation saved up. But I'm afraid my budget is a little tight this year. Last time I traveled to India, and it costed me a fortune.

B: Come on! We're traveling on our own. It won't cost too much.

A: What kind of transportation do you choose?

B: By air. Now it is the low season, the round-trip air ticket between Xi'an and Lhasa is no more than one thousand yuan. We can take a high-speed rail to Xi'an first.

B: How long are you going to stay in Tibet?

B: Two weeks. You can lay back and do nothing, just enjoy the sunshine in Lhasa.

A: Then count me in. Where will we stay?

B: The youth hostels are comfortable and cheap. We can save some money for delicious local specialties.

A: Then make sure that you book me a bed, too.

B: I'll take care of it.

A: Great! Oh, one more thing, don't forget to check the weather before we go. Be sure to take enough clothing.

B: No problem. Now let's make a list for what we need to take with us.

A: Perfect. I'm really looking forward to the coming week.

## Ⅳ Chinese Stories

### China Overview

China is one of the world's four ancient civilizations, and the written history of China dates back to the Shang Dynasty (1600-1046 B.C.), over 3000 years ago. As the world's third largest country, China covers a land area of 9.6 million square kilometers and a sea area of over 4.7 million square kilometers. With its 4 municipalities, 23 provinces, 5 autonomous regions and 2 special administrative regions, China will always remain united, and is home to approaching 1.4 billion people.

China is located in eastern Asia along the western shore of the Pacific Ocean, bordering the East China Sea, Yellow Sea, and South China Sea. In addition to over

18000 km of coastline, China has borders with Afghanistan, Bhutan, Myanmar, India, Kazakhstan, North Korea, Kyrgyzstan, Laos, Mongolia, Nepal, Pakistan, Russia, Tajikistan, and Vietnam.

The topography of China varies greatly from highly mountainous regions to inhospitable desert zones and flat, fertile plains. It can be compared to a staircase descending from west to east, with high plateaus, deserts in the west, plains, deltas, and hills in the east. The highlands and hill regions account for 67% of the country's total land area, and there are more than 2000 lakes dotting the landscape.

Known as the roof of the world, the Qinghai-Tibet Plateau is more than 4000 meters above sea level and forms the highest part of the country (the first step). The Himalayan mountain range has a number of peaks over 7000 meters, with the tallest in the world, Mount Everest at 8848.43 meters above sea level, at the Sino-Nepalese border, melting snows from these peaks are the source of several Chinese rivers including the Yangtze River and the Yellow River which run from west to east.

The second step is the Inner Mongolia and Yunnan-Guizhou Plateau as well as the Tarim, Sichuan and Junggar basins. The third step is the plains of the Yangtze River and of northern and eastern China, these areas are the country's most populated areas and the agricultural center of the country.

Rivers flow from west to east into the Pacific Ocean except a few in southwest China that flow to the south. The nation's largest rivers originate on the Qinghai-Tibet Plateau and thus have a high drop. With a length of 6300 kilometers, the Yangtze River is the largest river in China. The Yellow River, the second largest river in China, is also the birthplace of ancient Chinese civilization.

The vast territory of China spans nearly 50 latitudinal degrees, and most of it is in the temperate zone, with a small part extending south into the tropical and subtropical zones and the northernmost tip close to the Frigid Zone. China is a world-renowned monsoon region, where most parts are cold and dry in winter, and hot and rainy in summer.

Unlike other large countries, China only has one time zone. The Beijing time zone is 8 hours ahead of Greenwich Meantime (GMT +8). Daylight saving time is not observed.

As a large united multi-ethic country, China is composed of 56 ethnic groups. With a population of 1.4 billion, the Han Chinese account for 91.59% of the overall Chinese population and can be found in almost every part of China. The other 55 ethnic groups make up the remaining 8.41%. They are distributed extensively throughout different regions of China. The regions where they are most concentrated are Southwest China, Northwest China and Northeast China. The greatest number of ethnic groups can be found in Yunnan Province (25 ethnic groups). Zhuang has the largest population (more than 16 million) of ethnic groups. In order to ensure that the

56 Chinese ethnic groups live together in harmony, the Chinese government introduced a series of policies including ones to secure the equality and unity of ethnic groups, give regional autonomy to ethnic groups and promote respect for the faith and customs of ethnic groups. Together with the Han people, the Chinese ethnic groups are making great efforts to build a prosperous China.

China enjoys great language diversity. Mandarin is the official Chinese and is taught in schools all over China. But there are many dialects. Cantonese, for example, is spoken in Guangdong, Guangxi, Hong Kong, and Macao. Some around Shanghai, Zhejiang and Jiangsu speak Wu dialect. These dialects can be very different from Mandarin.

China boasts a huge depth of culture developed in a long and relatively isolated history, including Confucianism and other philosophy, tea culture, martial arts, poetry, calligraphy, the imperial legacy, and many others.

China has no unifying religion, but people hold a wide range of beliefs. From atheism or ancestor worship to one of the four major religions: Buddhism, Taoism, Islam, or Christianity.

With an annual growth averaging 9%, China has had the fastest growing economy for the last 30 years. It has developed at record speed to become the second largest economy in the world by GDP that stood at $15.73 trillion in 2020. China's poverty alleviation has shown the world a unique solution and has lifted about 100 million people out of poverty for the past 8 years. Guided by the theory of "lucid waters and lush mountains are invaluable assets", China is making great progress in ecological conservation. China is committed to the joint construction of the Belt and Road Initiative and the development of a community of shared future for mankind. China's goal is to create a better world and deliver better lives for all people.

### Tourism Industry in China

Tourism is a burgeoning industry in China since the beginning of reform and opening in the early 1980s. The Chinese tourism market has transformed into one of the world's most-watched inbound and outbound tourist markets. With rising standards of living, the tourism industry in China experienced a substantial growth spur over the last decade.

Tourism industry has become the main source of tax revenue and the key industry for economic development. According to China's Ministry of Culture and Tourism, the total revenue of Chinese travel and tourism industry amounted to 6.63 trillion yuan ($954 billion) as of 2019, a rise of 11% over the previous year. The industry contributed 2.1% to China's **Gross Domestic Product** (GDP) and provided around 28.25 million jobs. The impact of tourism on the employment market in China is even larger if indirect employment is taken into account. Direct and indirect employment in the travel and tourism industry in China totaled 79.87 million people, accounted for

10.3% of total employment population.

China registered a spike in **domestic tourism** with 6 billion trips in 2019, up 8.4% year-over-year. The **inbound tourism** market registered an increase with 145 million overseas visits made in 2019, up 2.9% year-over-year. According to the United Nations World Tourism Organization (UNWTO), 65.7 million foreign visitors entered the country in 2019, generating over $131.3 billion in revenue. China is now the fourth most visited country in the world, behind France, Spain and the United States. About 75.9% of the foreign visits were from Asia, and 35% of those foreign visits are for leisure and sightseeing. Myanmar, Vietnam, South Korea, Russia, Japan, the United States, Mongolia, Malaysia, the Philippines and Singapore are the top 10 source markets for China.

For **outbound tourism**, Chinese tourists made about 155 million visits to overseas destinations in 2019, a rise of 3.3% year-over-year. Spending of Chinese outbound travelers reached approximately $255 billion. The most popular travel destination for young Chinese travelers is Europe with a share of 61%, followed by Japan and South Korea. The leading international travel destinations of the mass market in China are Canada, Singapore, Australia, Japan and the United States.

China boasts a large number of attractions such as historical sites and relics, economic hot spots and a culturally diversed ethnic minorities. By the end of 2019, China has 55 world heritage sites, including 37 cultural sites, 14 natural sites, and 4 cultural and natural heritages. From the Great Wall to the Terra-cotta Army, and from sprawling mountain valleys to neon metropolises, there is something here for everyone.

## V Listening

**1. Listen to the dialogue and fill in the blanks.**

### Meeting Guests at the Airport

A: tour guide　　B: Mr. Jackson

A: _____, but are you Mr. Jackson from _____?

B: Yes, I am David Jackson. And you are...

A: I'm Wang Lei, _____. You can call me Edward. Nice to meet you! _____

B: Nice to meet you, Edward! _____.

A: It is my pleasure. _____, Mr. Jackson?

B: David, call me David! On the whole, _____.

A: _____. First let's go to hotel and

扫码
听听力

have a rest. _____, is it right?

B: Yes. That's right.

A: Hello, everyone! Welcome to Guilin! _____?

B: Yes, everybody is here with their luggage.

A: Could you put your luggage together here? _____.

B: That's splendid!

(After counting)

A: _____, right?

B: Yes.

A: Well, _____. Shall we go now?

B: _____. Yes, everyone is here. Let's go.

A: Attention please, everyone. _____.

**2. Listen to the dialogue and judge true (T) or false (F) for each statement.**

### Job Interview

1. Lily is going to graduate in the coming June. (　　)

2. Lily has been working as a part-time tour guide for two months. (　　)

3. Lily thinks that working as a tour guide is a hard job. (　　)

4. A tour guide needs to have some cultural background of his customer. (　　)

5. Lily wants to work in this travel agency on account of the high pay. (　　)

6. Lily gets the job. (　　)

## Ⅵ Speaking

**1. Discussion: Discuss the differences between traveler and tourist. Take notes and share with others in your own words.**

| Comparison between traveler and tourist | | |
|---|---|---|
| | Traveler | Tourist |
| Transportation | | |
| Hotel accommodation | | |
| Food | | |
| Size of the group | | |
| Local culture | | |

## 2. Role play: Work in pairs and act out the following dialogues.

(1) Xiao Jin is a student majoring in tourism management. He meets a foreign student Mike in the campus. They are talking about tourism development in their own country.

(2) Two friends are talking about the tour plan in the coming summer vacation.

(3) Jack is going to graduate this summer. He tries to apply a post as a bellman in a hotel. The human resource manager is interviewing him.

## 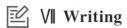 VII Writing

### Resume

#### 1. Writing Skills

A resume is a list of a person's qualifications for a job. The purpose of a resume (along with your cover letter) is to get an interview. A perfect resume has to be accurate and correct, free of grammatical and spelling errors. A resume should include the following key information:

(1) Your personal data / information: name, gender, date of birth, height, weight, health status, address, phone number, email address, etc.

(2) Your career objective / position wanted / job objective.

(3) A listing of jobs held, in reverse chronological order; start by talking about your job experience. It's your chance to bring attention to the most impressive part of your resume.

(4) Education, training or related experience; emphasize the skills you have which make you particularly suitable for the job.

(5) List of certifications, licenses or language spoken.

(6) List of accomplishments, awards, nominations or honors.

#### 2. Sample

| Resume | | |
|---|---|---|
| Name: Wang Lei | Gender: Male | Nationality: Zhuang |
| Birthday: 22/12/1999 | Place of birth: Guilin | Height: 178cm |
| Health: Excellent | Phone number: 139 * * * * * * * * | Email: wanglei@gltu.cn |
| Career objective: tour operator | | |

| |
|---|
| Education & Training |
| 2017-2021    Tourism management in Guilin Tourism University. (Course completed: Introduction to hospitality industry; Introduction to Travel Service Management; Tourism Marketing; Tourists Psychology) |
| 2014-2017    Guilin High School |

| |
|---|
| Work Experience |
| 2019-2020    Tour guide internship at CITS Guilin branch |
| 2018-2020    Part-time waiter at Sheraton Guilin Hotel |

| |
|---|
| Awards & Honors |
| 2019    The first prize in English Speech Contest |
| 2018    Excellent Student Cadre |

| |
|---|
| Special Skills: Fluent in Cantonese; excellent in Microsoft applications, Adobe Photoshop |

| |
|---|
| Self Appraisal: Team work spirit, good presentation and communication skills, be able to work under great pressure |

## 3. Writing Practice

You are applying for a position as a receptionist in a five-star hotel. Try to write a resume by filling in the following form.

| Resume | | |
|---|---|---|
| Name: | Gender: | Nationality: |
| Birthday: | Place of birth | Height: |
| Health: | Phone number: | Email: |
| Career objective: | | |
| Education & Training | | |
| | | |

| Work Experience |
| --- |
| |
| Awards & Honors |
| |
| Special Skills: |
| |
| Self Appraisal: |
| |

## Ⅷ Supplementary Reading

**Grand Tour**

Young English elites often spent months or years traveling around Europe to complete their education of a gentleman, in an effort to broaden their horizons and learn about language, architecture, geography, and culture in an experience known as the Grand Tour. The custom flourished from about 1660 until the advent of large-scale rail transport in the 1840s, and was associated with a standard itinerary.

Generally accepted itinerary is a long stay in France, especially in Paris, almost a year in Italy, and then a return by way of Germany and the Low Countries Netherland, Belgium and Luxembourg via Switzerland. With nearly unlimited funds, aristocratic connections and months (or years) to roam. They commissioned paintings, perfected their language skills and mingled with the upper crust of the

Continent.

## Gap Year

According to the Oxford Dictionary's definition, gap year is a period, typically an academic year, that a young person spends working and/or traveling abroad, often between leaving high school and starting university. To put it differently, it is the time during which one gets to pursue his or her interests while taking a break from the general course of studies or work. One can make the most of this time by exploring a different land, engaging in different kinds of meaningful as well as learning journeys, pursuing their passion, indulge in knowing more about the people and their lives as well as connect to other travelers, thus widening their social network. It is the time for you to learn and roll, cook and hike, dive and jump, volunteer and love.

## Red Tourism

Red tourism is related to historical sites and places which record China's revolution led by the Communist Party of China from 1921 to 1949. Because both China's National Flag and the Communist Party flag are red, the Chinese named these historical sites red scenic spots. In China, the red scenic spots are especially popular around the Party's Day (July 1, the anniversary of the founding of the Communist Party of China). China has 33315 revolutionary sites and relics on record. Statistics show that more than 800 million red tourism trips are made on average every year. Yan'an, Shaoshan, Nanchang, Jinggang Mountain, Zunyi are five most popular red tourist destinations.

## World Tourism Organization

The United Nations World Tourism Organization (UNWTO) is the United Nation's agency responsible for the promotion of responsible, sustainable and universally accessible tourism. It is the leading international organization in the field of tourism, which promotes tourism as a driver of economic growth, inclusive development and environmental sustainability and offers leadership and support to the sector in advancing knowledge and tourism policies worldwide. It encourages the implementation of the Global Code of Ethics for Tourism to maximize the contribution of tourism to social-economic development, while minimizing its possible negative impacts, and is committed to promoting tourism as an instrument in achieving the United Nations Millennium Development Goals (MDGs), geared towards reducing poverty and fostering sustainable development.

## Horse above Dragon Sparrow

"Horse above Dragon Sparrow" is a bronze horse, which was discovered in an

Eastern Han Dynasty tomb in Gansu province on the old Silk Road in 1969. The horse is poised as if it is flying and one of its hooves rests lightly on a dragon sparrow, a god of the wings, suggesting in a beautiful and imaginative way the almost divine power, which the Chinese people at that time believed the horse to possess.

It was chosen as the emblem of China's tourism industry in 1983 by National Tourism Administration(Now the Ministry of Culture and Tourism). It indicates a promising future of China's tourism industry. Horse is an important transportation tool in ancient China that means visitors can enjoy themselves in every corner of China. The emblem is a copperware representing China's 5000 years splendid culture and history appealing to worldwide visitors.

**Multiplier Effect**

Multiplier Effect is a concept borrowed from economics and used in tourism industry, which refers to the stimulus that an external source of income has on economy. It is an effect in which an increase in spending produces an increase in national income and consumption greater than the initial amount spent. Multiplier Effect signified that every dollar spent by a tourist circulated in a community a number of additional times before it leaves the community. For example, a tourist spends a dollar on an attraction, and then part of that dollar pays an attendant's salary. The attendant then uses his portion of that same dollar to buy food at the local supermarket. There is no certain number for how many times the multiplier effect works until the dollar leaves the community, however, common estimation ranges from 3 to 7 times.

## IX Check List

| Key Words | | | | |
|---|---|---|---|---|
| tourism | hospitality | accommodation | recreation | entertainment |
| transportation | sightseeing | restaurant | hotel | usual environment |
| vacation | tourist | waiter | receptionist | tour operator |
| concierge | butler | bartender | barista | tour leader |
| bellman | attendant | sommelier | chef | leisure time |
| travel agent | therapist | housekeeper | holiday | disposable income |
| inbound | outbound | topography | population | paid leave |
| mandarin | dialect | civilization | poverty | time zone |

**Useful Sentences**

1. Tourism is not a single entity.
2. Travel can be dated back thousands of years ago.
3. In the ancient Rome, lots of people traveled for commercial or sanative or religious purposes.
4. The greatest growth in international tourism has taken place only since the end of the Second World War.
5. In 2018, Guilin received over 100000000 visitors.
6. Tourism in its modern sense, began with the building of the railroads in the 19th century.
7. The first tour in the modern times was put together / organized by Thomas Cook in England in 1841.
8. By the end of 2019, China has 55 world heritage sites, including 37 cultural sites, 14 natural sites, and 4 cultural and natural heritages.

# Unit 2
# Tourist Transportation

**Learning Objectives**

After learning this part, you should be able to:

1. understand the role that transportation plays in the development of tourism industry.

2. discuss the advantage and disadvantage of different means of transport.

3. be familiar with the procedure of going through immigration and customs.

4. understand "Chinese mordernization" by introducing the great achivements in China's transportation industry.

 | Lead In

Classify the following words into corresponding categories.

| coach | ferry | helicopter | limousine | boat |
| yacht | train | jet plane | bicycle | high-speed rail |
| raft | metro | taxi | charter flight | motorcycle |
| cruise | light rail | car | shuttle bus | maglev |

| Air transport | Land transport | Water transport |
| --- | --- | --- |
|  |  |  |
|  |  |  |
|  |  |  |

## Background Reading

**Tourist Transportation**

As tourism involves the movement of people from their places of residence to the places of tourist attractions, the transport industry is clearly one of the major components of the tourism infrastructure. Without transport, travel (except by walking) would be impossible. Since the beginning of time, people have been traveling by various modes, from on foot to riding in a supersonic aircraft. Tourism and transportation are inextricably linked—indeed, it is difficult to overstate the importance of transportation in tourism. Studies have shown that tourists spend almost 30% to 40% of their total holiday expenditure on transportation and the remaining on food, accommodation, and other activities.

Modern technology became a major force in travel with the development of the steamship, locomotive, automobile, and airplane. These new forms of transportation put long-distance travel within the reach of more people than ever before by decreasing the amount of time and money necessary to take long trips. Mass tourism could not have existed without inexpensive and easily accessible transportation. Almost all the destinations in the world depend a great deal on efficient means of transportation being made available to tourists.

Transport not only provides the means of travel to the destination from the tourist's place of residence, and backs again, but also provides the means of traveling around the destination. Sometimes transport can be a main feature of a trip when the form of transport itself is one of the main reasons for taking the trip.

**Air Transportation**

Air travel has changed the way people view time and distance. Distance is now measured in hours and not in kilometers. The world has indeed shrunk and becomes a small village. The development of air transport mostly occurred after World War Ⅰ and Ⅱ. The first commercial service created for travelers was introduced by KLM, the Dutch Airlines, in 1920 between Amsterdam and London. Aircraft with the jet engines was introduced in the 1950s. In the year 1958, Pan American introduced the Boeing 707 services between Paris and New York. Due to the introduction of jet flights, the year 1959 onward saw a tremendous increase in air traffic. The concept of chartered flights was also introduced during this year.

Jumbo jets have revolutionized travel. The airplane was a boon to the tourism industry that made affordable mass transportation over long distance possible.

Transcontinental and transoceanic flights can carry several hundred passengers on each flight.

In 2019, the world's airline industry numbers 1715 airlines, 44600 aircraft, 3670 airports, 28.6 million scheduled departures, and carries 4.59 billion passengers. In the United States alone, commercial aviation generates more than $150 billion in annual revenue and employs over 550000 people.

Although a large number of people travel by air because of the speed, comfort, and economy in terms of time saved, there are negative aspects for those who wish to travel by air. These include some people's fear of flying and a lack of geographic accessibility, since many communities in the country are not served by air transportation. An additional problem is the length of time spent getting to and from the airport. Frequently, this time exceeds that spent en route.

**Rail Transportation**

The railway is the most economical, convenient, and popular mode of travel especially for long distance travel all over the world. The railroad was invented in the seventeenth century in Germany with wooden tracks. The first steel rail was developed in the USA during the early 1800s. When the first railways were built in the 1820s, it was easier for people to travel between towns, so they started to go for holidays by train. And some started to have holidays in the countryside as cities became larger, noisier and dirtier.

High-speed trains have lower energy consumption per passenger mile than air or automobile modes of transportation. They can move passengers at speed far faster than cars. Although they do not travel as fast as jet planes, they have advantages over air travel for relatively short distances (300 miles) because of the time required for the journey to the airport, checking in, going through security screening, and arriving in the city center. China, Japan and France have been the major leaders in high-speed rail.

Railways have promoted tourism by introducing a special tourist train. Trains can provide a romantic and intriguing way to spend a holiday. Top tourist trains such as the Palace on Wheels in India, Blue Train in South Africa, Glacier Express in Switzerland, Orient Express in France and Austria, Trans-Siberian Railway in Russia are a few of the world-class trains.

**Road Transportation**

Most of the travel in the world takes place in the automobile. In the United States, auto travel is an integral part of the travel industry with the vast majority 79% of US domestic person-trips taken by car, truck, camper/recreation vehicle, or rental car. Affordability, flexibility, convenience, and personal control make auto travel the most popular mode of transportation all over the world.

The key feature of the automobile is immediate accessibility and convenience. The automobile owner can leave from his or her own doorstep at any hour of the day or night and travel to a chosen destination. When two or more persons travel by automobile, the cost of travel per person is more favorable than it is with the other transportation modes.

Taxi and limousine service plays an exceedingly important part in tourism. Local transportation companies perform vital services for air, bus, rail, and cruise lines. Businessmen and tourists would have a difficult time getting from place to place if these services were not available. Streetcars, trolleys, and aerial trams serve as a form of taxi service and are of a special interest to visitors in tourist destination areas as a form of recreation and sightseeing.

Although tourists use planes, trains, motor coaches, taxis, shuttle buses, boats, and cruise ships to arrive at destinations, other modes of transportation are also an integral part of tourism. One of the most important and easily overlooked travel is pedestrian travel, or walking. Tourists and locals alike depend on their feet as a primary mode of travel. Tourists are great walkers, covering many miles sightseeing or using their feet to arrive at an attraction, sidewalk cafe, or gelato (ice cream) stand. Thus, it is imperative that pedestrian environments, the surface where tourists walk, and the areas in which they move are welcoming and safe. Tourism planners must make pedestrian travel part of their development plans.

Cycling is another mode embraced by some travelers and tourist destinations. Trams, cable cars, gondolas, and ski lifts are all additional modes of transportation that are important to specific resorts and destinations. They facilitate the flow of tourists and in many cases bring them to places that would otherwise be inaccessible. Also, they can be tourist attractions themselves.

## Water Transport

The water transport is regarded as the world's oldest mode of transport. It is the most energy-efficient and cheapest mode of transport over long distances. It is not only a way to travel but also a tourism experience. Travel by ship was the only means for traveling overseas until the middle of the twentieth century. Water transportation is only classified in two different categories, and these include both inland and ocean water transportation. There are various types of water vehicles. These include cruise ships, racing boats, off-road riding boats, windsurfer boats, riverboats, jet skis, battleships, raft boats, canoes, ferries, yachts, submarines, as well as tugboats.

Water transport today plays two main roles in travel and tourism, namely ferrying and cruising. The cruise lines are the new attraction among the tourist. The cruises are booked several months in advance for trips into the tropical and subtropical waters of the Hawaii, Caribbean, Mediterranean, etc.

Water transportation is also used in riverboat travel. The Mississippi River has been a popular tourist river since the first settlers came to the USA. Today, tourists enjoy two or three-day luxury trips along the river. In Europe, the Rhine, winding through the grapes growing areas of Germany, offers similar leisure tourist trips.

Motorized ferries and launches are used over rivers to transport tourists and locals, to transport vehicles, and offer facilities such as car parking, restaurants, viewing decks, etc.

##  III Situational Dialogue

### ➢ Dialogue 1

#### Check-in at the Airport

Scene: Airport staff (A) is receiving a guest (B) who is checking in at the counter.

A: Good afternoon, sir, may I help you?

B: I would like to check in for the flight to San Francisco. May I have an aisle seat?

A: I'll arrange it for you. May I have your passport, sir?

B: Sure. Here you are.

A: Do you have any luggage to check in?

B: Just one, please.

A: Do you have any power banks, lithium batteries, or sharp objects in your bag?

B: No, I don't.

A: Would you please put it on the scale?

B: OK. They are not overweight, are they?

A: I'm sorry, there is 2 kilograms over. On transcontinental flight to San Francisco, your free luggage allowance is no more than 23 kilograms each.

B: That's too bad. It must be the heavy overcoat I take in case of the chilly summer in San Francisco.

A: Sir, you don't have any carry-on luggage, you can take it out of your luggage and take it with you.

B: Good idea.

(After 5 minutes)

A: Sir, here are your passport and boarding pass. Your luggage claim tag is attached to the boarding pass. Your flight leaves from Gate B20 and boarding begins at 6:00 p.m..

B: How can I find Gate B20 from here?

A: After going through immigration and the security check, take the escalator to the international departure lounge on the second floor, use passenger conveyer or keep walking to the left and follow the signs. You won't miss it.

B: Thank you very much.

A: You're welcome. Enjoy your flight!

## ➢ Dialogue 2

### At the Immigration Counter

Scene: Immigration officer (A) is receiving a guest (B) at the immigration counter.

A: Passport, please.

B: Here it is.

A: What is the purpose of your visit?

B: I'm here for sightseeing.

A: How long will you be staying in China?

B: 10 days.

A: Where will you be staying during your visit?

B: I'll be staying in Guilin hotel. Here is the confirmation letter of my hotel reservation.

A: Do you have return ticket to San Francisco?

B: Yes, here it is.

A: Thank you. Enjoy your stay in China.

## ➢ Dialogue 3

### At the Customs Counter

Scene: At the customs counter, a customs officer (A) is checking a guest's (B) luggage.

A: Do you have anything to declare?

B: No, nothing that I know of. I have only my personal belongings. Just my clothing, camera, and a couple of gifts.

A: Are you bringing in any liquor?

B: No, I'm not.

A: Are you bringing in any cigarettes?

B: I take some tobaccos, but only for my personal use.

A: Is there any fresh food, live plants or animals in your bag?

B: No, there isn't.

A: Would you please make a record of your US currency?

B: Sure.

A: It is cleared. Enjoy your trip in China.

## ➢ Dialogue 4

### At the Information Desk

Scene: An information clerk (A) is answering questions from a guest (B).

A: Good afternoon, welcome to Guilin. Can I help you?

B: Yes. How can I get to Guilin Hotel in city downtown?

A: You can choose from airport shuttle bus or taxi.

B: How often does the shuttle bus run?

A: The airport shuttle bus departs for the city center every half an hour and you can transfer to a taxi which can get you to the hotel directly, or you can take a taxi which will cost you about 120 yuan.

B: I think taxi will be more convenient. By the way, could you tell me how I can get access to the Internet if there is no WiFi.

A: You can buy a local SIM card with your passport. They have special phone plan for foreign travelers.

B: Great. Where can I buy this kind of phone card?

A: The telecom company counter is over there.

B: Thank you very much.

A: With great pleasure. Enjoy your stay in China.

## IV Chinese Stories

### Travel in China

Transport in China has experienced major growth and expansion since 1949 and a comprehensive transportation system was constructed, combining flights, trains, highways and waterways, as well as local city transportation, such as taxi, public bus and metro. Even Tibet, one of the most inaccessible regions in the world, can be reached by train since the operation of Qinghai-Tibet Railway project.

**China Air travel**

China airlines have witnessed dramatic improvements since 1979, and there are over 1000 domestic and international airlines operated throughout the country. Beijing, Shanghai, Hong Kong, Guangzhou, Kunming and other provincial capitals have become regional aviation hubs, which not only have domestic flights to other parts of China, but also international flights to major cities of the world. Due to the huge distances in China, taking a plane is often the most convenient way to travel if you have limited time.

By the end of 2022, China has over 250 airports. The gigantic Beijing Daxing International Airport (PKX), with the impressive shape which has given it the nickname "Starfish", is the biggest airport in the world. The airport's design is pioneering while its location on the southern suburbs of Beijing is ideal in order to serve the Chinese capital and the neighboring areas of Hebei and Tianjin. There are currently 4 runways (with the prospect of becoming 7 runways in the future) and a vast terminal building covering a 700000 $m^2$ area while the ground transportation center extends to 80000 $m^2$. The new mega-airport hub is expected to handle up to 45 million passengers per year by 2021 and reach an outstanding 100 million in the future.

## China Train Travel

Railway transport is the primary form of national transportation in China, mainly for long-distance passenger travel and moving large quantities of goods. Taking trains is the most environmentally friendly way to travel in China and it is a great way to see parts of China you would not usually visit! You can choose high-speed trains or regular trains that are mainly sleeper trains and can often take 1-2 days.

China has the second longest and busiest rail networks in the world as well as the world's most extensive high-speed rail network in the world. By the end of 2022, China's railway network length has covered 150,000 km, including 42,000 kilometers of high-speed rail lines in service. Over 500 cities and towns can be reached by advanced and modern high speed bullet trains which are comfortable, secure, efficient, convenient, environment-friendly, and run at speed of 250 km/h ~ 350 km/h. The first China high-speed rail offering 350 km/h services was the Beijing-Tianjin Intercity Railway, which has been in service since August 1, 2008. It's easy to cancel or alter, if necessary. Unlike the high delay rates of airplanes and normal speed trains, high-speed trains have a high punctuality rate. This type of train is less affected by weather conditions or traffic control. It also has priority over a normal-speed train on the same railway line.

Today, railway networks in China remain at the stage of expansion and renewal. China's "four vertical and four horizontal high-speed railway network" has almost been completed, making China the world's first country with a complete high-speed rail network in operation. In addition, a 2000 kilometers network of intercity railway will be formed in economically developed and densely populated areas. A total of 3000 kilometers of branch lines will be expanded, offering a "seamless" transfer experience.

## China Highway Travel

Traveling by highway is another choice to reach your destinations in China. Instead of taking flight or high-speed train, travelers who visit by highway can appreciate scenery along the way, breathe some fresh air and have a taste of the real China and enjoy close contact with Chinese people. China highway is a network and an integrated system of national and provincial-level highway. The system of national-level highway is known as the 7918 network, composed of 7 radial highways from the capital Beijing, 9 north-south highways and 18 east-west highways. The highways in China have a total mileage of 177,000 kilometers by the end of 2022. Great efforts are being made to construct more expressways.

## China Waterway Travel

China has more than 5800 rivers with a total length of 400000 kilometers. Among the total length, China has 110000 kilometers of navigable rivers, streams, lakes, and canals, more than any country in the world. Taking cruise sailing along the rivers is not only a means of transportation, but also a relaxing and enjoyable way for sightseeing in China. Famous China Waterways & Cruise include Yangtze River cruise, Li River cruise, Beijing-Hangzhou Grand Canal and Huangpu River cruise.

## China's Subway

Taking metro is a cheap and green way to explore in the city. China's first subway system has been in operation since 1969 in Beijing. By the end of 2022, travelers can use subway in more than 50 cities of China. Among all the cities, Shanghai has got the longest length of 840 kilometers for metro rails with 20 lines opened. The average daily ridership of the metro in Shanghai is over 10 millions and account for 60% of Shanghai public transport. It is a good choice to getting around these cities by using metro way, which can save traveler's time and money. There are many English signs inside the subway station as well as a scan machine.

## China's City Bus

Most Chinese cities operate dozens of city bus lines in downtown and suburbs, offering convenient alternatives to metro. These lines can be identified either by numbers or Chinese characters representing the terminals. Automatic reporter in mandarin, local dialect and English announces city bus stops of most downtown lines.

## China's Taxi

Taxi is fast and convenient to take you to the destinations like hotels, airports, railway station and scenic spots, and the cost is really reasonable indeed compared with that in Europe and North America. Generally, it is not very hard to hail a cab along the street. However, the situation may be troublesome during rush hours (7:00-10:00 & 16:00-19:00) and at large passenger distribution centers like airports, railway stations, and long-distance bus stations.

**China Biking**

With once the nickname—the kingdom of bicycles, there are many people biking in the cities, counties and villages before. With the development of public transportation, biking is not as popular as before, but still available on the streets.

 Ⅴ **Listening**

**1. Listen to the dialogue and fill in the blanks.**

### At the Car Rental Counter

A: clerk of car rental company    B: guest

A: Good morning, sir. How can I help you?

B: I'd like to _____.

A: Certainly. Do you have a reservation?

B: No, I'm afraid I don't.

A: _____?

B: Let's see... We're two adults. _____?

A: Yes, we have. We've got a Ford for $89.90, including tax. You get 800 kilometers free. Then _____.

B: That sounds reasonable.

A: We have a _____ this weekend. For $3.00 more per day, you can _____. And, for only $5.00 more per day, you can _____. Would you like to take advantage of either of these offers?

B: No, thank you. I think this Ford will be fine.

A: May I _____?

B: Here you are.

A: Would you like _____?

B: No, thanks. I won't need any insurance. My credit card covers it.

A: Can you sign this agreement in these three places, please? Be sure to _____ or you'll be charged $3.00 per gallon.

B: Okay, I'll do that.

A: Here is your contract. Your car is _____. Just show your paperwork to the employee at the gate as you exit the parking lot. _____?

B: Yes, I'd like one. Thanks.

A: Here you are. _____.

B: Thanks. I appreciate it.

**2. Listen to the dialogue and judge true (T) or false (F) for each statement.**

Taxi Service

1. The guest needs to go to the airport to catch a flight. (　　)
2. There is a roadwork near the central avenue. (　　)
3. The taxi driver will detour to avoid the traffic. (　　)
4. The guest has no luggage. (　　)
5. The fare is $14. (　　)

扫码
听听力

## Ⅵ Speaking

**1. Discussion: Discuss the advantages and disadvantages of different means of transportation with your partner. Take notes and share with others in your own words.**

| The Advantages and Disadvantages of Different Means of Transportation |||
|---|---|---|
| | Advantages | Disadvantages |
| Airplane | | |
| Train | | |
| Automobile | | |
| Ship | | |

**2. Role play: Work in pairs and act out the following dialogues.**

(1) At the airport, Wang Lei is meeting the guests from Australia. He tries to identify them and greet them.

(2) At the railway station, Jack is trying to buy a ticket to Shanghai. Help him and tell him how to take the train.

(3) Jack wants to go to Wuhan from Guilin in the coming holiday. Wang Lei recommends transportation for him.

## Ⅶ. Writing

### Welcome speech

**1. Writing Skills**

A good welcome speech can extend the tour guide's thanks and welcome to the visitors. To deliver a welcome speech, a tour guide should

(1) express his/her warm-hearted welcome and extend his/her greetings to the tourists who have just arrived;

(2) introduce himself/herself, the driver and the travel agency he/she works for;

(3) express his/her wish to provide quality service;

(4) inform the tourists of hotel in which they are to stay, its location and facilities; he/she may also give a brief introduction to the scenic spots that the tourists plan to visit;

(5) try to take this chance to wish the tourists a good time during their stay.

The following two aspects should be observed while writing a welcome speech:

(1) the language in the speech should be clear, polite and interesting.

(2) the speech should express appreciation for the presence of the visitors on the occasion and be relevant to the cultural background of the listeners or tourists.

**2. Sample**

Good afternoon, ladies and gentlemen,

Welcome to China! Welcome to Guilin! Confucius, our great ancient philosopher once said, "What a great joy it is to have friends from afar!" Today, with such great joy, on behalf of the China International Travel Service Guilin Branch and my colleagues, I'd like to extend a warm welcome to all of you. Please allow me to introduce myself. My name is Wang Lei. You can call me Rick. I will be your local guide during your stay in Guilin. This is Mr. Wang, our driver. He has more than 12 years of driving experience. So you can be assured that your time on the bus will be safe and comfortable. Mr. Wang and I will do everything to make your visit a pleasant experience. If you have any problems or special requests, please don't hesitate to let us know.

Right now I'd like to take a minute to familiarize you with the area and explain tomorrow's travel schedule … I hope you would enjoy it.

Tonight, you're going to stay at Sheraton Guilin Hotel, a luxurious, five-star hotel with a good view of Li River. Since you are going to stay in our city for three days, we will be using the same coach during your stay in Guilin. So please take the trouble to jot down the plate number for future convenience: AC-1052, I will repeat: AC-1052. Got it? In case you get lost, I have my mobile phone on for 24 hours. My mobile telephone number is 13907736688. Don't hesitate to contact me whenever you are in need. It will take us 50 minutes to get to the hotel. Just have a rest. I'll let you know when we arrive at the hotel. Thank you!

**3. Writing Practice**

Write a welcome speech and give your presentation to the class.

## VII Supplementary Reading

### Accessibility

Accessibility is the means of travel to the destination. It refers to how easily visitors can get to your place. In tourism, accessibility is a function of distance from centers of population, which constitute tourist markets and of external transport, which enables a destination to be reached. It is measured in terms of the distance traveled, the time taken or the cost involved. However, accessibility can also refer to your destination's infrastructure, way finding, and ability to cater to visitors with disabilities. Access to transport embraces two components: arriving and leaving the destination as well as travelling whilst at the destination.

### Yangtze River

Winding across 6363 km of China, the Yangtze River is China's longest river and the third longest river in the world. It begins its journey at the Qinghai-Tibet Plateau, passes through 11 provinces and regions, and ends at the East China Sea.

Yangtze River has always been an important means of transport for goods into and out of China's interior because the river allows ship transport all the way to Chongqing. It is the most important river for agriculture, industry, and inland travel.

The Three Gorges Dam is the World's largest hydroelectric power plant which generates power that is equivalent of 15 nuclear plants, solved the centuries-old problem of devastating floods and allowed navigation well into the interior.

### The Yellow River

The Yellow River originates from the Roof of the World (the Qinghai-Tibet Plateau) in the Bayan Har Mountains in western China. It flows through nine provinces in the dry north of China: Qinghai, Sichuan, Gansu, Ningxia, Inner Mongolia, Shanxi, Shaanxi, Henan, and Shandong, before flowing into the Bohai Gulf at the city of Dongying. The Yellow River is the cradle of Chinese civilization, the spiritual home of the Chinese people.

The Yellow River is 5464 km long, the second longest river in China after the

Yangtze River and the third longest river in the world. The Ordos Loop is the characteristic rectangular "n" shape that the Yellow River takes round the city of Ordos in Inner Mongolia, as it deviates 600 km north, 300 km east, and then 600 km south.

**Beijing-Hangzhou Grand Canal**

Beijing-Hangzhou Grand Canal is the longest man-made river in the world. With a total length of 1801 kilometers, the canal starts from Beijing, passing through Tianjin and the provinces of Hebei, Shandong, Jiangsu and Zhejiang to the city of Hangzhou, linking five waterways, including Hai River, Yellow River, Huai River, Yangtze River and Qiantang River. With a history over 2500 years, the Grand Canal is still in use today.

**Low Cost Airlines**

LCA's (Low Cost Airlines) or LCLF (Low Cost Low Fare) carriers has been a major development in scheduled services in the last decade. A low cost airline operates on the basis of efficiency and generally has many features that differentiate it from the traditional carriers. These features include ticketless travel, online ticket sales, no international office, no frequent flyer points, no free food and beverage, no free check-in luggage allowance, no club lounge, use of secondary city airport. Southwest Airlines, which began service in 1971, is LCA's biggest US success story. It has been a model that other low-cost carriers have emulated. There are many low-cost airlines operating in Europe and the rest of the world. Air Asia, Norwegian, EasyJet, Ryanair are the most successful low cost airlines.

**Cruise**

Although ships have been a means of transportation since early times, the cruise industry is young. A cruise ship is a passenger ship used for vacations and pleasure trips, which is usually very large, and able to accommodate hundreds to thousands of people. Its purpose is to provide a resort experience rather than point-to-point transportation. While on the trip, most cruise ships stop at various ports where passengers are allowed to leave the ship and spend the day exploring an area. Most cruise ships have come to resemble floating cities. Though different cruise lines offer different amenities, cruising is often all-inclusive, and includes not just round-the-clock meals, but daily and nightly entertainment, various pools, fitness facilities, games and other fun activities, shopping, and even some adventure-type activities such as a rock wall or surfing simulator right on the cruise ship.

## IX Check List

| Key Words | | | | |
|---|---|---|---|---|
| helicopter | jet plane | stopover | jet lag | terminal |
| metro | subway | maglev train | light rail | road trip |
| driver's license | taxi | hub | shuttle bus | coach |
| cruise | yacht | ferry | parking lot | limousine |
| passport | visa | immigration | customs | declare |
| duty-free | baggage | luggage | suitcase | carousel |

### Useful Sentences

1. What is the purpose of your visit?
2. How long will you be staying in China?
3. Where will you be staying during your visit?
4. Do you have anything to declare?
5. Do you have any liquor or cigarette?
6. Is there any fresh food, live plants or animals in your bag?
7. You'll have to pay duty on this.
8. The camera is for personal use.
9. Is there an airport bus to the city?
10. Where is the bus stop(taxi stand)?
11. Where can I get the limousine for Hilton hotel?
12. Can I have a youth hostel list?
13. May I have a city map?
14. You have a number of options to get you there.
15. It'll take you two and a half hours by car.
16. You can rent a car right here at the airport.
17. You can take a subway to Shanghai Railway station.
18. You can take the high-speed rail to Guangzhou.
19. There is regular airport shuttle service.
20. You can drop off the device at the airport.
21. We have all kinds: compact, mid-sized, SUV, full-sized, luxury, and a minivan.
22. There's a 24-hour emergency number to call if you need assistance.
23. All of our cars have unlimited miles.

# Unit 3
# Travel Agency

**Learning Objectives**

After learning this part, you should be able to:
1. understand the role of travel agency and OTA.
2. understand what and how to give travel information.
3. help plan a tailor-made tour according to guests' time and needs.
4. understand the importance of the Belt and Road and a community with a shared future for mankind.

## Ⅰ. Lead In

Rank the correct SOP of travel inquiry.

a. Inquire the guest's idea about the destination, time to travel, number of travelers, etc;

b. Leave your contact number and express your wishes to offer assistance anytime in the future;

c. Greet and welcome the guest;

d. Introduce the tour package offered by the travel service according to guest's need;

e. Take a note of guest's name and contact number if possible;

f. Introduce the destinations and attractions;

g. Give guest travel brochure for further information.

Correct procedure: _____

## Background Reading

### Travel Agency

**Travel agency** is involved in developing, preparation, marketing and reservations of inclusive tours and individual travel packages. The fundamental role of a travel agency can be broadly summarized as: information, distribution, reservation and services. Travel agency combines all the components of a tour, including accommodation, transportation, restaurants, attraction visits, guiding services and so on to make up a holiday and sells it to the public through his own company, through retail outlets, or through approved retail travel agencies. They advertise and produce brochures to promote their products, holidays and itineraries. Niche tour operators may specialize in destinations, e.g. Italy, activities and experiences, e.g. skiing, or a combination thereof.

Travel agency forms an essential bridge between travel suppliers and customers. They purchase service from the principals in large quantities and create different packages that are tailored to families, singles and couples within a definite time period. They buy in bulks and secure considerable discounts from the suppliers that could not normally be matched by customers buying directly.

A **package tour** is a pre-arranged combination of not fewer than two of the following tourism services when sold or offered for sale at an inclusive price and when the service covers a period of more than 24 hours or includes overnight accommodation.

A **travel agent** is thus an expert, knowledgeable in schedule, routine, lodging, currency, prices, regulations, destination, and can give up-to-date and accurate information regarding various services and general information about travel. Travel agents need to be outgoing and approachable, with excellent customer service skills.

For a typical business day, a travel agency's functions include:

1. Arranging transportation—air, sea cruise, bus, rail, car rentals locally and abroad;

2. Preparing individual itineraries, personally escorted tours, group tours and selling prepared package tours;

3. Arranging hotels, motels, resort accommodations, meals, sightseeing, transfers of passengers and luggages between terminals and hotels, as well as special events such as music festivals and theatre tickets;

4. Handling and advising on the details pertaining to travel and baggage insurances, foreign currency exchanges, documentation requirements (visas, health certificates, etc);

5. Using professional know-how and experience in the provision of air, train and other transportation schedules, hotel rates and their standards as well as qualities;

6. Arranging reservations for special-interest activities such as religious pilgrimages, conventions and business travels, incentive and educational tours, ecotour and gourmet tours, sporting/adventure trips, etc.

## OTA

With the rapid development of information technology and the universal popularity of Internet, travel shopping via online agencies has become very popular. **OTA or Online Travel Agency** quickly occupied the tourism market with its features of convenience, efficiency, high response and personalization, especially in the last minute segment and also because of the frequent usage of the smart phones. Today consumers are on-the-go and the advantage of a booking system and the reservation solutions provided by OTA is that it offers instant payment and booking confirmation.

OTA is an online company whose website allows consumers to book different travel services directly via the Internet. Some examples of OTA are TripAdvisors, Agoda, Expedia, priceline, Ctrip. Travelers can check for hotel reviews, search for interesting places nearby and even look at different pictures taken by travelers for a review before they decide to travel there. Priceline and Expedia are the two largest OTAs in the world and they have been around for 20 years. Being able to provide personalized experience is what wins customers and keeps them coming back.

In the first quarter of 2023, the transaction volume of the Chinese online travel booking market amounted to 787.5 billion yuan. Ctrip is the biggest Online Travel Agent in China, with 65% of the country's online travel market. Ctrip officially changed its corporate name to "Trip.com Group Limited" on October 25, 2019. The group operates a family of travel brands, which mainly consists of Trip.com, Ctrip, Skyscanner, and Qunar. In Western countries, it is better known under its Trip.com brand. The platform is particularly popular among young, trendy and aspirational middle-class travelers who like to put together their own trips and itineraries, rather than relying on guided tours. In fact, 70% of Ctrip's users are these Free Independent Travelers (FITs). Ctrip users can use the platform to book everything from hotels and flights to entertainment, dining out and travel services. Other online platforms include Filggy, a leading OTA platform operated by Alibaba, and Tongcheng, Tuniu.

The rapid development of Internet and the mobile Internet also cause the explosive growth of the customized travel industry. The development of SaaS technology has also greatly improved the efficiency of the designers. The designers are important providers of customized services. Their thoughts, creativity, and experience are hard to be replaced by technology.

The original reason of tour operating was the difficulty for ordinary folk of making arrangements in far-flung places, with problems of language, currency and communication. Traditionally, the travel industry focused on the travel agency sales channel. Customers used to visit their local travel agencies, and purchase travel tickets or gather vacation information through the agencies. The advent of the Internet has led to a rapid increase in self-packaging of holidays. However, tour operators still have their competence in arranging tours for those who do not have time to do DIY holidays, and specialize in large group events and meetings such as conferences or seminars. Also, tour operators still exercise contracting power with suppliers (airlines, hotels, other land arrangements, cruise companies and so on) and influence over other entities (tourism boards and other government authorities) in order to create packages and special group departures for destinations that might otherwise be difficult and expensive to visit.

## ‖ Situational Dialogue

### ➤ Dialogue 1

#### Inquiring About Package Tour

Scene: Wang Lei (A), a travel agent of Sunshine Travel Service, is receiving a guest (B) who is interested in traveling abroad.

A: Good morning. What can I do for you?

B: I am thinking of traveling abroad in the coming National Day holiday.

A: How many people will be traveling with you?

B: We have a group of four. My parents will be traveling with us.

A: Do you have any destinations in mind?

B: We've been to Thailand, Singapore, Malaysia and Japan. We would like to visit a country that doesn't need a long flight. I am open to suggestions at this point.

A: Do you enjoy warm weather, or are you looking forward to a cooler vacation?

B: A nice temperate climate would be best for me.

A: Have you ever been to Cambodia? There is a 5-day-4-night charter flight package tour on sale. A direct flight from Guilin to Siem Reap only takes 2 hours.

B: That sounds good.

A: Here is the brochure for Cambodia. Take a look, please. We will spend three days in Siem Reap for the famous world's cultural heritage: Angkor Wat.

B: What is included in the package?

A: The round-trip air tickets between Guilin and Siem Reap, four nights accommodation in five-star hotels and all the meals during the tour. We'll also pay for a three-day admission ticket for Angkor Wat.

B: Do we have any opportunities to try some local food?

A: Sure. Some local specialties have been arranged in our itinerary.

B: What extra fee do we need to pay when we arrive?

A: Only the tips for the tour guide. That's 3 US dollars a day.

B: How much is the tour?

A: The total price is 2880 yuan for each person.

B: Thanks very much for your information. I'll talk about it with my family.

A: You're quite welcome. Here is my business card. Please feel free to contact me if you have any questions.

➢ **Dialogue 2**

**Giving Information About Tailor-made Tour**

Scene: A travel agent (A) is receiving a guest (B) who is inquiring information about tailor-made tour because he wants to spend his vacation in a very relaxing way.

A: Good afternoon. Can I help you?

B: Yes, I want to travel abroad with my family in the winter vacation. But I am not interested in your package tours, since all of them have such a tight schedule. I wonder whether you have anything special for customer like me.

A: Certainly. We cater to all age groups and to different tastes, including independent backpackers, couples, families, and student groups. We specialize in creating private tours, customized according to your own needs and interests.

B: It seems that you are what I'm looking for.

A: Do you have anything special in mind?

B: I just like a place where my family can enjoy the natural beauty and delicious local food. What's more, somewhere warm. Where do you suggest?

A: Have you ever been to Bali Island?

B: No. I've heard of it before. It is in Indonesia, isn't it?

A: Yes. It is. The idyllic Indonesian island is a beautiful combination of spirituality, natural beauty and a taste of the exoticism. Next month will be the perfect time to visit there. I highly recommend it.

B: I wonder whether there are good hotels there.

A: Yes, there are a lot of five-star hotels along the beach and most of them enjoy a fantastic sea view. There are a lot of water sports you can choose, such as diving, snorkeling, surfing and so on.

B: Sounds interesting. Could you book flight tickets and hotel rooms for us?

A: Certainly. We can also offer tour guide service and local transportation if you like. Our travel adviser can offer a one-on-one service and design the itinerary just for you. All details will be professionally considered.

B: Great! I would like to discuss the itinerary with my wife.

A: No problem. Here is the brochure for Bali Island. Could you friend me on WeChat? It's convenient to contact me if you need more information.

B: OK. Goodbye.

A: Have a nice day!

##  IV Chinese Stories

### Silk Road and The Belt and Road

**Silk Road**

Silk Road, also called Silk Route, was a historic ancient trade route across the Afro-Eurasian landmass that connected East, South, and Western Asia with the Mediterranean and European world, as well as parts of North and East Africa.

It was used regularly from 130 B. C. when the Han Dynasty officially opened trade with the west, to 1453, when the Ottoman Empire boycotted trade with the west and closed the routes. The original Silk Route was established during the Han Dynasty by Zhang Qian, a Chinese official and diplomat. The Silk Route was popular during the Tang Dynasty, from 618 to 907 A. D. Travelers could choose among a number of land and sea paths to reach their destination. The routes evolved along with territorial boundaries and changes in national leadership. Trade grew and declined, and it reached a height when the Mongols had control of Eurasia from the Yuan Empire (1279-1368) to Eastern Europe. The fall of the Yuan Empire and the growth of maritime trade ended Silk Road trading. It was dubbed the Silk Route because of the heavy silk trading that took place during that period. This valuable fabric originated in China, which initially had a monopoly on silk production until the secrets of its creation spread.

Originating at Xi'an, the 4000-mile (6400 km) road, actually a caravan trail, followed the Great Wall of China to the northwest, bypassed the Takla Makan Desert, climbed the Pamirs (mountains), crossed Afghanistan, and went on to the Levant; from there the merchandise was shipped across the Mediterranean Sea. It stretched from Asia to the Mediterranean, traversing China, India, Persia, Arabia, Greece, and Italy, linking China with the West, that carried goods and ideas between the two great civilizations of Rome and China. Trade along the Silk Road included fruits and vegetables, livestock, grain, spices, leather and hides, tools, religious objects, artworks, precious stones and metals and other items of value. The greatest value of the Silk Road was the exchange of culture. Art, religion, philosophy, technology, language, science, architecture, and other elements of civilization were exchanged along these routes, carried with the commercial goods the merchants traded from country to country.

The Venetian explorer Marco Polo (1254-1324) traveled on these routes from Italy to China, which was then under the control of the Mongolian Empire, where they arrived in 1275. The explorer spent 24 years in Asia, working in Kublai Khan's court, perhaps as a tax collector. Marco Polo returned to Venice, again via the Silk Road, in 1295, just as the Mongolian Empire was in decline. His journeys across the Silk Road became the basis for his book *The Travels of Marco Polo*, which gave Europeans a better understanding of Asian commerce and culture.

But he is not credited with naming them. Both terms for this network of roads were coined by the German geographer and traveler, Ferdinand von Richthofen, in 1877, who designated them 'Seidenstrasse' (silk road) or 'Seidenstrassen' (silk routes). Polo, and later von Richthofen, make mention of the goods which were transported back and forth on the Silk Road.

Symbolizing communication and cooperation between the East and the West, the Silk Road Spirit is a historic and cultural heritage shared by all countries around the world.

## The Belt and Road

The Belt and Road is an initiative, which was launched by President Xi Jinping in 2013, to focus on improving and creating new trading routes, links and business opportunities with China, passing through over 60 countries along the way, across Asia, Europe, the Middle East and Africa. The project involves building a big network of roadways, railways, maritime ports, power grids, oil and gas pipelines, and associated infrastructure projects.

One Belt, or The Silk Road Economic Belt, is primarily land-based and aimed to build a "Eurasian land bridge"—a logistics chain from China's east coast all the way to Rotterdam/Western Europe and develop a number of economic corridors connecting China with Mongolia and Russia, central Asia and South east Asia. Substantial progress has already been made. The first freight trains from Europe to China began running in 2011 and have cut transit time from Germany to China from 50 days by sea to 18 days.

One Road is called the 21st-Century Maritime Silk Road. It is a sea route rather than a road that connects coastal China to the Mediterranean via Singapore-Malaysia, the Indian Ocean, the Arabian Sea, and the Strait of Hormuz.

China has announced investments over $1 trillion in the various infrastructure projects and is funding them by offering low-cost loans to the participating countries.

The aims of the Belt and Road initiative is to develop prosperity for underdeveloped parts of China, particularly in the west of the country, to develop new opportunities for China to partner and cooperate with the various countries along the routes, many of which are developing countries, and to increased integration, connectivity and economic development along both routes.

## V Listening

**1. Listen to the dialogue and fill in the blanks.**

### Tour Inquiry

A: Hello, welcome to Universal Travel Agency! May I help you?

B: Yes, I'm _____.

A: _____?

B: I'm not sure. Somewhere warm. _____?

A: We _____. Is there any places possible you have never seen?

B: Sure. I haven't traveled much.

A: Have you ever been to South Africa? We _____. Take a look of the brochure.

B: Thank you!

A: Or how about Indonesia? We _____ for Indonesia. _____.

B: I haven't been to either of these places. But I don't know.

A: We also _____. Are you interested?

B: Oh, yes! _____?

A: I was there last spring. It was beautiful. _____.

B: OK. Let's _____.

**2. Listen to the dialogue and judge true (T) or false (F) for each statement.**

### Cruise Tour

(1) The guest is interested in a cruise tour on Yangtze River. (    )

(2) The cruise on Li River will take about 3 hours. (    )

(3) Lunch is not included in the tour. (    )

(4) The guest will go back to Guilin by bus at 5:30 p.m.. (    )

(5) Price for the cruise tour is 480 yuan. (    )

## Ⅵ Speaking

1. Discuss the differences between package tour and tailor-made tour with your partner. Take notes and share with others in your own words.

| Comparison of Package Tour and Tailor-made Tour | | |
|---|---|---|
| | Package Tour | Tailor-made Tour |
| Cost | | |
| Convenience | | |
| Freedom | | |
| Others | | |

2. Role play: Work in pairs and act out the following dialogues.

(1) Sam is a travel consultant. He is receiving a guest who is interested in the package tour to Gansu. Introduce the package tour and answer the guest's questions.

(2) Two friends are talking about their experience of using online travel agencies.

(3) Lily is a travel adviser providing customized travel for her guest. She is talking with a guest who wants to take a vacation abroad in the coming summer vacation with his family.

## Ⅶ Writing

### Itinerary

**1. Writing Skills**

An itinerary is what a travel agency proposes as a travel plan for its customers. Itinerary is mainly made up of three parts: 1. The arrangements for various activities in a journey according to the time sequence. 2. The service standard provided by travel agency: ①Transportation; ②Accommodation; ③Tickets for the tourist attraction; ④Tour guide. 3. Others: tour price, major scenic spots, precaution and insurance instruction, etc.

Tips for writing:

①An attractive title is indispensable for an itinerary.

②Itinerary should be written in a concise and appealing manner.

③Phrases such as present participles and gerunds are preferred to clauses in it.

Sample

| |
|---|
| Itinerary of a 8 days/7 nights Tour from Beijing-Huangshan-Shanghai |
| Day 1   Beijing<br>On arrival, CITS guide will hold a welcome sign to meet you at the airport. You will be transferred to the hotel on a room and breakfast basis. The rest of the day is free to relax. |
| Day 2   Beijing<br>Morning: Take a half-day tour to the Forbidden City that 24 emperors lived and ruled for over 500 years. The South Gate leads you to Tian'anmen Square—the biggest central square in the world.<br>Afternoon: Continue to visit the famous imperial garden—Summer Palace. (B+L) |
| Day 3   Beijing<br>Morning: You will take a half-day visit to the awesome Great Wall of China.<br>Afternoon: Continue to the Ming Tomb, the mausoleums of Emperors of the Ming Dynasty. And Walk along the Sacred Way, which means the road leading to heaven. (B+L) |
| Day 4   Beijing to Huangshan<br>Morning: Explore the Temple of Heaven, where ancient emperor worshipped God and prayed for harvest.<br>Afternoon: Transfer to take the flight to Huangshan. Meet the guide at the airport and transfer to the hotel. (B+L) |
| Day 5   Mount Huangshan<br>Have a full-day visit to Mount Huangshan Scenic Area by car and take the Yungu Cableway up to the mountain. Enjoy the spectacular view at Flower-scattering Valley, Lion Peak, Cloud-dispelling Pavilion, etc. Stay at the hotel on the mountain. (B+L) |
| Day 6   Huangshan to Shanghai<br>Morning: Watch the sunrise in the early morning. Continue enjoying the beauty of Mount Huangshan, going down the Mountain by Yungu Cableway. Explore ancient Hongcun Village, which listed as world cultural heritage sites by UNESCO.<br>Afternoon: Transfer to take the flight to Shanghai. Meet the guide at the airport and transfer to the hotel. (B+L) |

Day 7　Shanghai

Morning: Visit the Yu Garden, which is a famous Chinese classic garden.

Afternoon: Take a walk along the famous waterfront, the Bund, to fully appreciate this diverse city. Have a short cruise on Huangpu River where you could see grand buildings along the river. (B+L)

Day 8　Shanghai and Departure

Transfer to take the departure flight, or alternatively extend your stay. (B)

| Season | Group Size | Budget Class | Standard Class | Deluxe Class |
| --- | --- | --- | --- | --- |
| Peak | 1 traveler | $600 | $720 | $880 |
| Peak | 2-4 travelers | $450 | $580 | $700 |
| Peak | 5-9 travelers | $400 | $500 | $600 |
| Low | 1 traveler | $550 | $650 | $800 |
| Low | 2-4 travelers | $400 | $500 | $620 |
| Low | 5-9 travelers | $350 | $420 | $500 |
| Hotel Level | | 3 Star | 4 Star | 5 Star |
| Food Standard | | 8 dishes, 1 soup | 10 dishes, 1 soup | 12 dishes, 1 soup |

| Price include | Price exclude |
| --- | --- |
| 1. Entrance fees of all sites as mentioned; 2. Meals as listed in the itinerary, B=American breakfast; L=Chinese lunch; D=Chinese dinner; 3. Excellent private guide; 4. Private vehicle with driver; 5. Round transfers between airports or rail stations and hotels; 6. Hotels (twin share basis) as listed in the itinerary. Single supplement will be charged; 7. Domestic flights (Economy-class) or trains as listed, airports taxes and fuel charges; 8. Service charge & Government taxes. | 1. Personal expenses such as laundry, drink, telex, telephone calls or excess baggage charges; 2. China visa fees; 3. The international flight or train of entering and exiting China; 4. Any meals that are not specified; 5. Tips to guides and drivers. |

Peak Season: 03/01/2020-10/31/2020　　Low Season: 11/01/2020-2/28/2021

## 2. Writing Practice

Choose a destination and write a 4-day-3-night itinerary.

| Itinerary of a 4-day-3-night Tour |
|---|
| Day 1 |
| Day 2 |
| Day 3 |
| Day 4 |

| Season | Group Size | Budget Class | Standard Class | Deluxe Class |
|---|---|---|---|---|
| Peak | 1 traveler | | | |
| | 2-4 travelers | | | |
| | 5-9 travelers | | | |
| Low | 1 traveler | | | |
| | 2-4 travelers | | | |
| | 5-9 travelers | | | |
| Hotel Level | | | | |
| Food Standard | | | | |

## Ⅷ Supplementary Reading

**Road Trip**

A road trip, is a long distance journey on the road taken in a motor vehicle for pleasure, while discovering millions of places along your route, especially when the journey itself is part of the appeal. It is important to remember that the drive is the most important part of a road trip. Taking a road trip with your friends or family can be an excellent way to shed some old skin and live a little, destress and forget your troubles for a while, and to make some fond memories along the way. Don't be in a rush. If there is something interesting you would like to stop and see, do so. It is a part of the experience. It's also one of the rites of passage for those who live in a country long enough to make road trips truly exciting, such as the USA, Canada and China, at least one road trip in a lifetime is essential before you can truly feel that you understand the pulse of your country better.

**Toilet Revolution**

When foreigners visit China tourist areas, they complain about the issue of public toilets the most. Many foreigners said they will never forget the scary toilet experience. Given this fact, how could our tourism industry take big strides? On April 1, 2015, President Xi Jinping made important comments on toilet revolution and civilized tourism. The country launched the toilet revolution in 2015 to increase the number and sanitation of toilets at tourist sites. The campaign was expanded to improve public toilets in cities and build better toilets in rural areas. Since the toilet revolution was launched in 2015, China has seen much improvement in terms of the quantity and quality of tourist toilets. More than 30000 tourist toilets had been newly installed, renovated or expanded in China. Toilet improvement is not a trivial matter, it is key to the improvement of urban and rural environments. It should not be limited to scenic zones or urban areas, it should be extended to rural areas as part of efforts to revitalize the rural economy and improve rural living conditions.

**Lonely Planet**

*Lonely Planet* is the largest travel guidebook publisher in the world. After the *Let's Go* travel guide series that was founded in 1960, the *Lonely Planet* books were the second series of travel books aimed at backpackers and other low-cost travelers.

*Lonely Planet* was founded by married couple Maureen and Tony Wheeler. They met in London in 1970 and, in July 1972, they embarked on an overland trip through

Europe and Asia, eventually arriving in Australia in December 1972. *Lonely Planet's* first book, *Across Asia on the Cheap*, consisting of 94 pages, was written by the couple in their home. *Across Asia on the Cheap* offered the advice of amateur traveler and the brand is born after Tony mishears a mention of a "lovely planet" in Joe Cocker's song "Space Captain". The popularity of the hippy trail, combined with the success of the original *Lonely Planet* publications, led the Wheelers to further develop the brand they had founded. The couple discovered writers in bars and also told people that if they could return to Australia with a completed book, then *Lonely Planet* would publish it. The *Lonely Planet* guidebook series initially expanded in Asia, with the India guide book that was first published in 1981, but progressively became a dominant brand in the rest of the world. By 1999, *Lonely Planet* had sold 30 million copies of its travel guides and, by this stage, the company was recognized beyond hippie trail adventurers, and wealthier readers were an established part of the readership. By 2007, *Lonely Planet* had officially been classified as a "super brand", having published over 500 titles and had sold 80 million titles, translated into more than eight languages. A mention in a *Lonely Planet* guidebook can draw large numbers of travelers, which invariably brings change to places mentioned. *Lonely Planet* gives you the tools to plan your next trip: in-depth information on destinations, inspiring ideas on what to see and do. *Lonely Planet* believes that responsible travel can be a force for good. As a company, the only thing they want to do more than explore the world is protecting it for future generations of travelers.

Originally called "Lonely Planet Publications", the company changed its name to "Lonely Planet" in July 2009 to reflect its broad travel industry coverage and an emphasis on digital products. By 2017, *Lonely Planet* launches mobile App "Guides", reaching 1 million downloads and covering 100 cities.

## Hitchhiking

Hitchhiking (also known as thumbing, hitching, or autostop) is a means of transportation that is to travel by standing on the side of the road and stick out the thumb to ask for free rides from passing vehicles. Hitchhiking became a common method of traveling during the Great Depression.

Between 1964 and the mid-1980s, hitchhiking was part cheap transportation, part meditation. It was a way to see the country, to learn about one self, and to touch base with America. In the 1970s, hitchhiking was much more popular in affluent countries than these days. In the 1980s, hitchhiking experienced a clear decline in affluent countries in Western Europe and North America. The decline was attributed to a number of factors including lower air travel costs due to deregulation, the presence of more money in the economy to pay for travel, more numerous and more reliable cars, and a lack of trust of strangers.

Nowadays, hitchhiking is perceived as dangerous, and few drivers are willing to pick someone up. Police departments discourage it, and many states in the United States explicitly ban it.

## TripAdvisor

TripAdvisor is the world's largest travel platform, helps hundreds of millions of travelers each month make every trip the best trip. Travelers can share their travel experience in visual and written media. With this application, people can see millions of comments and photographs shared by travelers, share their own comments and experience, compare flight ticket prices, get information about tourist spots or businesses in their immediate environment and find answers for some specific questions on traveling. Travelers across the globe use the TripAdvisor site and app to browse more than 878 million reviews and opinions of 8.8 million accommodations, restaurants, experiences, airlines and cruises. TripAdvisor is available in 49 markets and 28 languages.

 ## Ⅸ Check List

| Key Words | | | | |
|---|---|---|---|---|
| travel service | attraction | destination | itinerary | package tour |
| schedule | route | brochure | admission | tailor-made |
| high season | low season | guide | tour leader | tour operator |
| currency | insurance | review | caravan | round-trip |
| scenic spot | road trip | hitchhiking | meal | charter flight |
| one way | direct flight | stopover | budget | vaccination |
| Useful Sentences | | | | |

1. What kind of tour do you have in your mind?
2. When are you planning on traveling?
3. How many people will be traveling with you?
4. Have you ever been to Cambodia?
5. We have two kinds: a seven-day package tour and a ten-day package tour.
6. Here is the brochure for Cambodia.
7. May I suggest to you our 3-day-2-night package tour to Beijing?

8. It includes round-trip air tickets between Guilin and Beijing and four nights' hotel accommodation and all the meals during the tour.
9. We will pay the admissions for the scenic and historical spots.
10. It will cover all the fees of the trip.
11. Children under 1.2 meters in height travel free, except for their meals and air tickets.
12. On the first day, they will visit ..., on the second day, they will tour ..., on the last day, they will visit ...
13. An English-speaking tour guide will accompany you to the five destinations.
14. We will pick you up just in front of the agency at 8:00 a.m. Sunday morning.
15. We specialize in creating private tours, customized according to your own needs and interests.
16. Next month will be the perfect time to visit there.
17. I highly recommend it.
18. We can also offer tour guide service and local transportation if you like.
19. Our travel adviser can offer a one-on-one service and design the itinerary just for you.
20. All details will be professionally considered.

# Unit 4
# Hotel Accommodation

**Learning Objectives**

After learning this part, you should be able to:
1. get some information about the hotel operation.
2. be able to communicate with foreign guests in different occasions in hotel.
3. describe the development of Chinese hotel industry.
4. understand occupational requirements for different jobs in hotel industry and develop your professional dedication and professional ethics.

## I Lead In

Put the following objects into appropriate place they belong to

| bathtub | minibar | projector | sheet | copy machine |
| stapler | towel | hairdryer | carpet | laser printer |
| pillow | toothpaste | wardrobe | bathrobe | air conditioner |
| mattress | faucet | shampoo | ashtray | laptop |

| Guest room | Bathroom | Business center |
|---|---|---|
|  |  |  |

## II Background Reading

### Introduction of Hotel Industry

Hotel is an establishment providing accommodation, meals, and other services for travelers and tourists. By most definitions, the hotel industry refers not only to hotels, but also to many other forms of overnight accommodation, including hostels, motels, inns and guesthouses.

It is the world's oldest commercial business. Facilities offering hospitality to travelers have been a feature of the earliest civilizations. Early traders travel from region to region to trade their spices, gold and exotic goods, they need places to sleep and eat while traveling. People built inns and taverns along the trade route. Guest rooms were first part of private dwellings. In Greco-Roman culture, hospitals for recuperation and rest were built at thermal baths. During the Middle Ages, various religious orders at monasteries and abbeys would offer accommodation for travelers on the road. The precursor to the modern hotel was the inn of medieval Europe. These inns would provide for the needs of travelers, including food and lodging, stabling and fodder for the traveler's horses and fresh horses for the mail coach. For a period of about 200 years, from the mid-17th century, coaching inns served as a place for lodging for coach travelers. Inns began to cater to richer clients in the mid-18th century. One of the first hotels in a modern sense was opened in Exeter, England in 1768. Hotels proliferated throughout Western Europe and and North America in the early 19th century, and luxury hotels, including the Savoy Hotel in the United Kingdom, the Ritz chain of hotels in London and Paris, Tremont House and Astor House in the United States, began to spring up in the later part of the century, catering to an extremely wealthy clientele. Today many lodging places provide meeting rooms, convention facilities and services, restaurants, bars, entertainment, gift shops, casinos, health clubs, and other activities and facilities.

Hotel operations vary in size, function and cost. Most hotels and major hospitality companies have set industry standards to classify hotel types. An **upscale full-service hotel** facility offers luxury amenities, full service accommodations, an on-site restaurant, and the highest level of personalized service, such as a concierge, room service and clothes pressing staff. Full service hotels often contain upscale full-service facilities with a large number of full service accommodations, an on-site full service restaurant, and a variety of on-site amenities. **Boutique hotels** are smaller independent, non-branded hotels that often contain upscale facilities with a unique environment or intimate setting. Small to medium-sized hotel establishments offer a limited amount of on-site amenities. **Economy hotels** are small to medium-sized hotel establishments that offer basic accommodations with little to no services. **Extended stay hotels** are small to medium-sized hotels that offer longer-term full service accommodations compared to a traditional hotel. A **motel** is a small-sized low-rise lodging with direct access to individual rooms from the car park.

Apart from the classification mentioned above, hotel are categorized by related authority according to facilities available, service coverage and service quality, as is known as "star" ranging from one to five.

Hotels operate 24 hours a day. For this operation to be successful, departments must communicate and work together to provide quality customer service to the guests. In modern hotels, all staff work is customer-oriented, even the establishments and facilities and organization construction are customer-centered. "Functional departments serve operational departments, while operational departments serve customers", this is becoming the motto of many hotels. What goes on behind the scenes should be invisible to hotel visitors, so they are ensured a pleasant stay and want to return on subsequent trips.

**The front desk** is a hotel's lifeline. Front desk staff members greet potential guests on the phone and arriving guests upon check-in. They set the tone for the complete guest experience. The front desk needs to be staffed 24 hours a day, typically in three shifts. In addition to taking reservations and performing check ins and outs, a front desk clerk addresses guest issues, provides information and serves as a communication hub for other departments. Day shift personnel complete check outs, accept new reservations and coordinate with housekeeping to manage the inventory of clean and available rooms. Evening shift personnel perform check ins, answer phones and take the hotel into quiet time. The overnight staff typically run the daily audits and work closely with security to ensure all guests are in a safe environment.

**The housekeeping department** is an integral part of hotel operations. Cleanliness of both guest rooms and common areas is imperative if a hotel is to provide a pleasant experience. Upon checkout, a guest room must be thoroughly cleaned. All bedding and bathroom linens must be removed and replaced with clean ones. Bathrooms must be sanitized and carpeting vacuumed. If a guest stays over, the bed must be re-made, fresh linens provided and floors vacuumed. Common areas in a hotel must also be cleaned on a daily basis. Hallways should be vacuumed and public bathrooms cleaned and re-stocked. Workout rooms, pool areas, meeting rooms and other areas should all be attended to as needed. At least once a quarter, heavy duty cleaning should be performed including laundering bedding, washing windows, turning mattresses, polishing floors and shampooing carpets. Room rental is a hotel's main business and its major source of profit. The day-to-day operation of the typical rooms department yield a departmental income of 70% or more, compared with 15% to 20% for **the food and beverage department**. Traditionally the hotel has looked at the occupancy as a measure of success. Another indicator of operational success is the average rate per rented room (**the average daily rate**, or ADR).

Most hotels provide some type of food and beverage, whether it is a full-service restaurant or a simple continental breakfast. A kitchen manager or chef creates menus and oversees the ordering, preparation and delivery of food. Depending on the extent of the restaurant operation, other staff may include sous chefs, prep cooks and dishwashers. A restaurant manager is responsible to hire, train and schedule appropriate wait staff. If the hotel also offers wedding and conference services, banquet sales and operations managers handle the bookings and manage the flow of the event.

Even the best quality utilities and electronics can break and malfunction. In today's tech-oriented world, there is also more to repair and fix in terms of computers, TV screens, game consoles, and other cutting-edge tech items than before. Depending on the size of the building, one or more full-time maintenance mechanics should be on staff. Expertise in plumbing, electrical and other mechanical issues is needed. The maintenance staff may also be responsible for the hotel grounds including landscaping, cleaning parking lots, snow removal and operation of outdoor pools and spas.

While the front desk may book reservations, marketing the property is necessary to drive business. A website is a necessity and should offer an online booking option. Many properties align with larger travel websites such as Priceline, Booking and Ctrip that offer booking opportunities. The marketing team must keep up-to-date with the latest marketing channels and practices, including social media, content marketing, OTAs(Online Travel Agency), and so on.

Successful operation of a hotel business is all about putting heads in beds and providing a good experience. Rapid technological advances have made a huge impact on the industry in more ways. It has been and continues to be difficult for hotels to keep up with the pace of development. However, the core business of the hotel industry has not changed significantly. Hotel guests in the 21st century may have different wants and needs to guests in the 18th century, but the basic principles of the accommodation and hospitality industry have remained the same.

 ||| **Situational Dialogue**

> **Dialogue 1**

### At the Front Desk

Scene: Mr. Jackson (B) and his wife come to the Reception Desk. The receptionist (A) is greeting them.

A: Good afternoon, sir and madam. What can I do for you?

B: We'd like to check in.

A: Do you have a reservation, sir?

B: Yes, I booked a room on your website two weeks ago. My name is David Jackson.

A: Just a minute, Mr. Jackson. I'll check the arrival list ... Yes, you've booked a double room with a view of Li River from today to April 20, is that right?

B: Exactly!

A: May I have your passports, please?

(The receptionist checks their passports carefully, prints the registration form and hands it to Mr. Jackson)

A: Thank you, sir. Would you please confirm the information and sign your name here?

B: All right. Let me take care of it ... Here you are.

A: Thank you. Mr. Jackson, You've booked a double room for three nights. The room rate is 980 yuan per night, plus a 15% service charge. According to our hotel policy, we will charge you 3000 yuan as deposit. How would you like to make the payment? We accept cash, credit card, Alipay and Apple pay.

B: Credit card, please. Here you are.

A: Thank you. Mr. Jackson, Your room number is 618. Here is your room card and credit card. Breakfast is served between 7:00 a.m. and 10:00 a.m. in the Western restaurant on the second floor.

B: Thank you. By the way, is there a spa service in your hotel?

A: Yes. The spa center is on the top floor and open from 10:00 a.m. to 10:00 p.m., you'd better dial 8 to make a reservation before your visit.

B: Thank you.

A: With pleasure. Wish you a most pleasant stay in our hotel.

## ➢ Dialogue 2

### Concierge Service

Scene: The bellman (A) helps the Jacksons (B) with their luggage and answers their questions.

A: Good afternoon, sir and madam. Welcome to Sheraton Guilin Hotel.

B: Good afternoon.

A: Very glad to have you here. Do you have any luggage?

B: Yes, they are all in the trunk.

A: So you've got three pieces of luggage altogether, is that right?

B: Yes, that's right.

A: Just a moment, please. I'll get a trolley. Sorry to have kept you waiting. After you, please. I'll show you to your room soon after you finish checking in at the Front Desk.

B: Thank you!

(10 minutes later)

A: Mr. and Mrs. Jackson, your room is on the 6th floor. This way to the elevator, please.

B: We've heard that the local fishermen often fish on Li River with cormorant. Is it true?

A: Yes, there is a cormorant fishing show at 8:00 p.m. in the evening. I can call to make a reservation for you if you like.

B: Could you book two tickets for tomorrow evening?

A: Certainly, I'll call to make the reservation and tell you the details later.

B: Thank you. It is dinner time. Could you recommend a good restaurant to us?

A: There's a Chinese restaurant on the second floor. There you can try different delicious food.

B: Sorry, we'd like to try a local restaurant.

A: Our hotel is located in the city center. The main attractions and the shopping area are all within walking distance. If you go to Central Avenue, you'll see about 10 different restaurants, all of which are highly recommendable.

B: Great! How do we get to Central Avenue from here?

A: When you exit the entrance of the hotel, turn left and walk for 2 blocks, and you'll come to Central Avenue. The restaurant zone is on the left side of the avenue. Would you like me to draw you a map?

B: Thank you. You are very thoughtful!

A: It's my pleasure.

## ➢ Dialogue 3

### Business Service

Scene: Mr. Jackson (A) is a business traveler staying in the executive floor. Now he is talking with a clerk (B) working in the guest service center by phone.

A: Good morning. Guest service center.

B: Hello, This is Mr. Jackson in room 618.

A: Hello, Mr. Jackson. How may I assist you?

B: I would like to have a meeting with my business partners tomorrow afternoon. May I use your meeting room?

A: According to our hotel policy, guests staying at the executive floor have 3 hours free use of meeting room per stay. May I know how many people will attend the meeting? And what time would you like to use the meeting room?

B: We have a party of 7 persons. I would like the meeting to be begun at 2:30 p.m..

A: OK. Mr. Jackson, The meeting room will be ready for you at 2:30 p.m. tomorrow afternoon. It is at the end of the corridor on your same floor. Do you need any special equipment?

B: Is there any multimedia devices in your meeting room? We may need to do some presentations.

A: No problem. All the meeting rooms are well equipped with modern multimedia devices.

B: That's great. By the way, could you arrange a tea break for us at 3:30 p.m.?

A: Certainly. Mr. Jackson, your afternoon tea is free. But I'm afraid your guests have to pay 88 yuan for the afternoon tea per person.

B: That's OK. Could you charge all the fees to my room? There's one more thing, I need 7 copies of a market survey. Could you send someone to pick it up here in my room?

A: Sure. I'll send someone up to your room immediately. Is there anything else I can do for you?

B: I think that's all.

A: OK, Mr. Jackson. You need a small meeting room for 7 persons at 2:30 p.m. tomorrow afternoon and a tea break at 3:30 p.m., 7 copies of the market survey will be delivered to your room later. Is that right?

B: Exactly. You are very helpful. Thank you.

A: It's my pleasure. We look forward to serving you tomorrow.

## ➢ Dialogue 4

### Making a Complaint

Scene: Mr. Jackson (B) is checking out at the front desk. He is making complaints to the Receptionist (A) about his unpleasant stay in the hotel.

A: Good morning. What can I do for you?

B: Hello there. I'd like to check out, please.

A: I hope you have had a pleasant stay at Sheraton Guilin, Mr. Jackson.

B: Actually, I'm afraid my stay hasn't been very pleasant at all.

A: I'm sorry to hear that. Is there anything that you would like us to look into?

B: I didn't get a good night's sleep at all last night.

A: I'm so sorry about that. Was there a problem with the room?

B: The room was fine and the bed was very comfortable, but there is something wrong with the air conditioning. It was ever so noisy.

A: I'm terribly sorry about that. I'll send someone up to your room to take a look at it right away.

B: Well, that is too late for me, isn't it? And your Internet connection also functions poorly. WiFi is so slow that it is impossible to send an email with a file.

A: I really apologize for all the inconvenience. I assure you this won't happen next time. Here is your bill, Mr. Jackson, please have a check.

B: Hold on a second. I have been charged for breakfast. This is absolutely ridiculous. I would like to speak to your manager.

## IV Chinese Stories

### Development of Chinese Hotel Industry

The earliest hotel accommodation in China can be dated back to the period of Yao, Shun, and Yu over 2000 years ago. Government-run posthouse appeared in Shang Dynasty along the road providing shelter for traveling military forces and government officials. In the Sui (581-618) and Tang (618-907) Dynasties saw a significant development of hotels, in number and size, which far surpassed any previous generation. The emergence of branding with the "presence of hotel signs everywhere" during the Yuan Dynasty (1271-1368) while during the Ming (1368-1644) and Qing (1644-1911) Dynasties the themed area of reception, restaurants and rooms was well established.

In the early phase of China's economic reform, the hotel sector was primarily orientated toward serving an overseas demand because hotel facilities of international standards were in short supply during the first decade of economic transition. The initial hotel projects of the late 1970s and early 1980s were developed as joint ventures between Chinese government agencies at national and local level and the Chinese diaspora. Examples included the Beijing Jian Guo Hotel, a joint venture between China International Travel Service Beijing Branch and an American Chinese. In 1983 and 1984, investors from Hong Kong developed the two famed hotels in Guangzhou, the White Swan Hotel and the China Hotel. It was reported that more than 50% of the inward foreign investment in China in the 1980s was invested in hotel development. The fact that the hotel sector in China was the earliest and most open industry to the outside world was attributed to the infusion of investment and transfer of management know-how from overseas investors.

The initially favored ways by which international companies entered the Chinese market was by management contracts and joint ventures. The first management contract was reached in 1982 between the Hong Kong-based Peninsular Hotel Group and the joint owners of Beijing Jian Guo Hotel. Then, gradually, international hotel firms entered the market by signing management contracts to operate the upscale and luxury hotels catering to overseas business and leisure travelers. By 1991, 202 hotels were counted as joint venture hotel projects with overseas investors, 215 hotels were reported under international management contracts and 4 hotels were financed completely by overseas investment.

In terms of hotel development, a key moment was the establishment of a star rating system in 1988, which for the first time in China permitted comparison and bench-marking of hotels across the nation. In 1991, the category "One Star"

accounted for 9.34% of the total stock of hotel rooms, but by the end of 2019 this figure was only 0.62%. In itself, this reflects the early nature of the resources available to the Chinese hotel industry in terms of its inheritance of basic facilities and the initial relatively low cost investments of early entrepreneurs responding to an embryonic growth in domestic demand. Equally the share of "Two Star" hotels has fallen in the same period from 33% to just 16.5%. However, for much of the period, "Two Star" hotels accounted for about one-third of the total stock of hotel rooms, and it is only since about 2008 that its share has radically fallen. At the other end of the scale, "Five Star" hotels have consistently retained about 7% to 10% of rooms throughout the thirty-year period. Equally "Four Star" hotels have significantly increased their share of the rooms from about 13% in 1991 to 26% in 2019. Taken with the increase in rooms to be found in "Three Star" hotels with a big share of 48.9% of total stock of hotel rooms, it is evident that the quality of hotel provision in China has not only increased in numbers of hotels, but also in rooms, with an accelerated growth rate in better quality rooms in recent years. A number of reasons account for this, one of which is the growing importance of international and domestic tourism.

The rapid development of China's domestic tourism can be attributed to structural changes in the national economy that have taken place since the start of the economic reforms. These changes include the rise in living standards, the increase in the number of public holidays, a growing demand for business related travel and a production sector shifted to service orientated businesses that include events and conferences. Demand for hotel accommodation has significantly changed over the past four decades in terms of volume and for better quality services and a greater variety of accommodation.

International hotel firms first entered the China market to serve the international tourists at mid and upscale levels. As the Chinese economy continued to sustain rapid growth, international hotel firms subsequently increased their presence in China to target both overseas and domestic tourism with more diversified lodging options ranging from luxury services to budget accommodations. Luxury brands such as Four Seasons, Ritz-Carlton, and Shangri-La are now found in major metropolitan markets, such as Shanghai, Guangzhou and Beijing. Marriott International has been focusing on both upscale and mid-market segments. Familiar brands such as InterContinental, Starwood, Accor, Hyatt, Hilton, etc, continue to expand in major and secondary cities and other tourist destinations. Market opportunities for budget and mid-market segments for the growing numbers of Chinese domestic tourists also attracted Wyndham (Days Inn, Super 8, and Howard Johnson brands) to expand operations in China.

After learning and absorbing international practices, domestic hotel firms developed rapidly after 1990. Jin Jiang Hotels and BTG Hotels are now ranked as the 6th and 9th largest hotel firm in the world respectively. Not only are these domestic firms growing in size, but many have strategically positioned themselves in different market segments through branding. For example, Jin Jiang Hotels has developed 31 brands to capture different travel motivations and lifestyles. Chinese companies have also moved into the budget hotel sector that has been generally avoided by the international hotel chains, and major brands include Home Inn, HanTing Inn, 7 Days Inn, Jinjiang Inn, Vienna, ect.

After the hotel properties are fully developed, Chinese hotels compete for market share by interactive marketing, impeccable guest services, brand management, guest relationship management, yield management and efficient technological applications in reservations and communications.

The Chinese hotel industry has formally adopted "Green Hotel Practices" as part of governmental policies relating to the issues of pollution and environmentally sensitive. As "pollution-free" has become an officially important standard to grade a hotel, the Chinese hotel industry has become increasingly aware of environmental protection. More and more hotels make security, health and no pollution as their top priorities in the construction of their hotel to spread the knowledge of environmental protection to customers.

## V Listening

**1. Listen to the conversation and fill in the blanks.**

### Check out

A: Good morning, reception. May I help you?

B: Yes. I am leaving right now. Could you _____?

A: Of course. May I have your room number, please?

B: Room 618.

A: All right. _____.

(At the front desk)

A: Good morning. Can I help you?

B: I'd like to check out now.

A: _____, please?

B: Here you are.

A: One moment, please... Mr. Jackson, _____, am I right?

B: Yes, that's right.

扫码
听听力

A: _____ ?

B: My wife and I just had breakfast at the dining room, but we paid the bill in cash.

A: Fine. I'll _____ . Here you are. The total is RMB 6680 yuan. Please have a check.

B: I'm sorry. What's this for?

A: That's _____ .

J: Oh, I see. _____ ?

A: Yes, that's everything. _____ , in cash or by credit card?

B: Credit card, please. Here is my visa card.

A: Mr. Jackson, _____ .

J: Oh, yes.

A: Thanks. Here is your card and receipt. We hope you enjoyed your stay with us here and that you'll have a nice trip home.

B: Thank you.

**2. Listen to the conversation and judge true (T) or false (F) for each statement.**

### Laundry Service

(1) Mr. Jackson want to wash his suit and shirt. (    )

(2) The laundry forms and bags are in the top left-hand drawer of the writing desk. (    )

(3) Mr. Jackson needs to get his laundry back that afternoon for an important appointment. (    )

(4) For express service, guest can get their laundry back in three hours. (    )

(5) The shirt must be washed by hand in hot water. (    )

## Ⅵ Speaking

**1. Discussion: Talk about the characteristics of different types of hotels with your partner. Take notes and share with others in your own words.**

| The Characteristics of Different Types of Hotels | | |
|---|---|---|
| | Commercial Hotel | Resort Hotel |
| Location | | |
| Facilities | | |

| Services | | |
|---|---|---|
| Others | | |

**2. Role play: Work in pairs and act out the following dialogues.**

(1) Mike would like to have a single room for tonight, but he hasn't made a reservation.

(2) Mr. Jackson comes to front desk to change some US dollars into RMB.

(3) The GRO (Guest Relation Officer) is showing a guest around the hotel and introducing hotel services and facilities.

# Ⅶ Writing

## A Reply to Complaints Letter

**1. Writing Skills**

A reply to complaints letter is mainly made up of three parts:

(1) Making an apology to the guest.

(2) The reasons why the guest made a complaint.

(3) The solutions to the complaint.

**2. Sample**

## A Reply to Complaints Letter

_____(写信日期)

_____(饭店名称及地址)

Re: _____(主题)

Dear _____(客人姓名),

I'm writing with reference to _____(投诉内容) dated _____(日期)。

Firstly, Please allow me to apologize to you, on behalf of our hotel, for all the inconvenience/ troubles caused by our carelessness.

We ensure you this matter will be managed properly to satisfy you, although due to _____(简述原因), we are sorry for having not met your expectations.

With regard to this, we have worked out a solution to this problem _____(解决方案), which we hope will be acceptable to you and make you satisfied.

Please contact us if you have any other requirements or proposals to our services or the management of our hotel.

Yours sincerely,
_____（签名）

### 3. Writing Practice

Mrs. Jackson is unsatisfied with the spa in the hotel. She doesn't think the service is good, and it charges unreasonable. Write a reply to her complaints letter.

## Ⅷ Supplementary Reading

### Bed and Breakfast

Bed and breakfast, or B&B, are smaller establishments, which offer guests private rooms for overnight stays, along with breakfast in the morning. Often, these establishments are converted from private homes and many B&B owners live in their property. Bed and breakfasts have been very popular with the traveling public in Europe for years. The abbreviation of "B&B" on roadside signs first became popular in the British Isles—typically with a detachable "Vacancies" sign swinging below. Tourists will see B&B signs in many windows there. While they are often a budget option, high-end or luxury B&Bs also exist. Today, B&Bs offer a warm and cozy alternative to the corporate hotel or motel. Most B&Bs pride themselves on being privately owned and operated, as well as offering accommodations in quaint and cozy homes in locations that offer historical, leisure or small town attractions.

### Motels

The history of the motel is directly linked to American car culture. The freedom it represented touched the American spirit of adventure, individualism and exploration. The concept of motels started with the establishment of the US interstate highway, which began in the 1920s. As highways were built, they enabled people to travel long distance much easily. During these long journeys, travelers found it impossible to find lodging in the suburbs (for hotels being located in city centers).

It is to cater to this need that motels sprang up. They were located by the interstate highways, in the suburbs, where travelers were provided with lodging and parking facilities, usually for an overnight's stay. The first motel in the world is the Milestone Mo-Tel of San Luis Obispo, (now named as Motel Inn), which was constructed by Arthur Heineman at a cost of ＄80000 in 1925. The word "Motel" came as part of a linking of the two words, "Motor" and "Hotel".

A motel is an establishment that provides travelers, motorists and vacationers the space and room for lodging and parking, where the rooms have direct access to the parking area. They are typically located by the roadside and offer ample free parking. A motel is what most people now go for when they have to make a booking for a night's stay in their journey. The main reason is motels offer good facilities just as hotels, but at much cheaper rates.

**Airbnb**

Airbnb is a peer-to-peer accommodation marketplace connecting hosts—vendors of rooms or accommodations—and travelers via its website. It doesn't own any real property but earns through processing fees. The simple business model made common people rent out their properties that would otherwise go unused. With its 150 million users, 640000 hosts, and four million listings in 65000 cities, Airbnb is now the world's largest hotel chain. You may enjoy the advantages such as access to a kitchen, more spaces, and some unusual or unique places to stay or living locally, walk down the street to the market or the local shops and interact with people as you buy your daily groceries. You may also risk your travel with problems like: You might not like your accommodation once you arrive. A host can cancel at the last minute. There are Airbnb issues around security and safety. Your experience will be more unpredictable. There may be safety issues, such as the lack of emergency exits or fire extinguishing equipment.

**Boutique hotel**

Boutique hotels are small hotels that have typically between 10 and 150 rooms in unique settings with upscale accommodations. Many boutique hotels are furnished in a themed, stylish or aspirational manner. The popularity of the boutique concept has prompted some multi-national hotel companies to try and capture a market share. They are also found in resort destinations with exotic amenities such as electronics, spas, yoga or painting classes. It has a strong personality. A boutique hotel's intimate size produces its one-on-one five-star hospitality service and its heady ambiance. Whether it's independently owned or a member of a luxury hotel brand or association, it has an independent attitude and works hard to not feel like a corporate hotel. It's rich in local flavor. Whether urban or rural, a good boutique hotel reminds you of where you are. Often, it conveys a strong sense of place and pride in its location's heritage.

**Ecolodge**

The term ecolodge refers to a type of accommodation located in a remote destination in nature. Generally eco lodges are equipped with less than 30 rooms.

They are designed to have minimal impact on the environment and to be as sustainable as possible in their usage of resources. They may prioritize the use of local products, adopt recycling measures, focus on energy saving and use sustainable bed linen and towels. Furthermore, they aim to improve the welfare of the local population by supporting local suppliers and workers.

Ecolodges in comparison to eco hotels and green hotels are located further away from civilization. They target ecotourists, by offering a nature-based experience. Often they are not impacted by noise, traffic, smog or pollution. Furthermore, to boost the experience and create awareness for the environment, many ecolodges have access to guides who are trained in biology or have significant knowledge of the habitat. They thereby allow guests unique insights into the surrounding habitat. In recent years, eco lodges have been growing in popularity due to the trend towards sustainability.

**Hostel**

Hostels provide budget-oriented, sociable accommodation where guests can rent a bed, usually a bunk bed, in a dormitory and share a bathroom, lounge and sometimes a kitchen. Rooms can be mixed or single-sex, and private rooms may also be available.

Hostels are often cheaper for both the operator and occupants; many hostels have long-term residents whom they employ as desk agents or housekeeping staff in exchange for experience or discounted accommodation.

There is less privacy in a hostel than in a hotel. Sharing sleeping accommodation in a dormitory is very different from staying in a private room in a hotel or bed and breakfast, and might not be comfortable for those requiring more privacy. Hostels encourage more social interaction between guests due to the shared sleeping areas and communal areas such as lounges, kitchens and internet cafes.

## IX Check List

| Key Words | | | | |
| --- | --- | --- | --- | --- |
| lobby | twin room | concierge | bellman | assistant manager |
| reservation | suite | upgrade | operator | business center |
| front office | confirm | credit card | payment | executive floor |

| available | guarantee | deposit | banquet | recreation center |
|---|---|---|---|---|
| view | signature | trolley | coupon | pick up service |
| elevator | corridor | attendant | linen | health club |
| luggage | sheet | pillow | towel | service charge |

**Useful Sentences**

**Registration**

1. Good morning, Sheraton Guilin hotel, can I help you?
2. We have various types of rooms: single rooms, double rooms, suites, and deluxe suites. What kind of room would you prefer?
3. Would you like a room with a view of the garden/river/sea/beach/courtyard?
4. How many nights are you going to stay?
5. What time will you be arriving?
6. We can only hold the room by 6:00 p.m..
7. A single room is $60 per night, excluding a 10% service charge.
8. The current rate is RMB 980 yuan per night. Breakfast is included.
9. Do you have a reservation with us, sir?
10. In whose name was the reservation made?
11. Just a moment, please. I will check the arrival list/ reservation record.
12. Sorry to have kept you waiting, sir, you have reserved a room from today to Friday.
13. I'll check. Let me see if there is a room available.
14. May I have your passport, please?
15. You should pay a deposit of $1000 in advance.
16. How would you like to settle your bill?
17. Here's the key to Room 908. Please keep it. The bellman will show you up.
18. Enjoy your stay.

**Concierge service**

1. Good afternoon, madam and sir. Did you have a nice trip?
2. Is this your first trip to Guilin?
3. This way, please.
4. Let me help you with your luggage.
5. How many pieces of luggage have you got?
6. The Reception Desk is straight ahead. After you, please.
7. One moment, please. I'll get a trolley.
8. Watch the steps.
9. Please take this elevator/lift to the 9th floor.
10. The room is at the end of the corridor.
11. Here we are, Room 618.

**Laundry service**

1. Excuse me. Have you any laundry?
2. Is this for pressing only?
3. Usually laundry received before 11:00 a.m.. It will be returned by 7:00 p.m..
4. I am afraid it is too late for today's laundry.
5. Is your dress colorfast?
6. We will do our best to remove the stain on your coat.
7. Would you like express service or same-day?
8. If you need express service, you can get it back in four hours, but there will be an extra surcharge of 50%.
9. Here is your laundry, sir. A skirt, a jacket, and a pair of trousers.
10. A valet will be up in a few minutes.

**Business service**

1. All the meeting rooms are well equipped with modern multimedia devices.
2. How many copies would you like?
3. Here is your original.
4. Would you like me to staple these for you?
5. Shall I staple them on the left side or at the top?

**Maintenance service**

1. The air conditioner/TV/heating system isn't working.
2. I'm awfully sorry for that, sir. I'll see to it right away.
3. I'll speak to the person in charge and ask him to take care of the problem.
4. What seems to be the trouble?
5. I'll call the Maintenance Department right away.
6. We'll send a repairman/electrician/plumber/chambermaid/bellman immediately.
7. I'll fix it for you.
8. I do apologize for the inconvenience. Please wait just a few minutes.
9. I'm sorry. We can't fix it today. I am afraid you have to change to another room.
10. A bellman will help you with your luggage.
11. It's working now.
12. Everything is all right now.

# Unit 5
# Food and Beverage Service

**Learning Objectives**

After learning this unit, you should:
1. get some knowledge about food and cooking.
2. acquire the knowledge of Chinese and Western cuisine.
3. be able to communicate with foreigners in a restaurant.
4. be able to introduce Chinese food culture to foreign guests and develop a strong cultural confidence and a virtue of diligence and thrift.

## Lead In

Classify the following words into corresponding categories.

| ham | pumpkin | fork | ginger | sandwich |
| macaroni | toast | pancake | vinegar | cabbage |
| sausage | French fries | mushroom | butter | eggplant |
| soy sauce | spinach | chopsticks | popcorn | carrot |
| curry | bacon | spoon | ketchup | broccoli |
| mustard | asparagus | saucer | cucumber | knife |

| | |
|---|---|
| Food | |
| Condiments | |
| Table wares | |

## Background Reading

### Food Service Industry

The food service industry is a very old business. Such service came out of the early inns and monasteries. With the development of stagecoaches, taverns began providing food and lodging along the roads and in small communities.

The food service industry consists of restaurants, travel food service, and vending and contract institutional food service. Local restaurants are made up of establishments that include fast-food units, coffee shops, specialty restaurants, family restaurants, cafeterias, and full-service restaurants with carefully orchestrated "atmosphere". Travel food service consists of food operations in hotels and motels, roadside service to automobile travelers, and all food service on air planes, trains, and ships. Institutional food service in companies, hospitals, nursing homes and so on is not considered part of the tourism industry.

Travelers contribute about $130 billion to food service sales each year, whether for a coffee shop breakfast, a dinner on an airline, a sandwich from a bus station vending machine, or a ten-course dinner on a cruise ship. Travelers, including foreign visitors, spend more money on food than anything else except transportation, and travelers account for about one fourth of the total sales in the food service industry.

Menus can be of two types, **a la carte** and **table d'hote**. The a la carte menu consists of a complete list of all the food items being offered on that day. The patron then chooses the individual items desired. In table d'hote, a combination of items is chosen.

Over the past two decades, the food and beverage business has grown at a phenomenal rate. This has been especially true for fast-food companies. Although the fast-food segment is the most rapidly growing segment, the high-quality segment of the restaurant industry must not be overlooked. Much of this business is based on customers seeking a special or different experience in dining out. Local entrepreneurs who emphasize special menus, varying atmospheres, high-quality food and service have most effectively satisfied this demand. New concepts or trends include ethnic restaurants, especially those with an Asian or Mexican flavor; increased demand for health foods, fish, local produce, and regional dishes; and variety in portion sizes.

Although dining out is common among tourists and food can be the major driver in deciding when and where to travel, **culinary tourism** is a relatively new niche and has come into its own in the last decade. Culinary tourism is the pursuit of unique and memorable culinary experiences of all kinds, often while traveling, but one can also be a culinary tourist at home. Wikipedia defines culinary tourism or food tourism as experiencing the food of the country, region, or area, and it is now considered a vital component of the tourism experience.

Food is also considered a part of cultural tourism and is linked to agritourism. Wine tourism, whiskey tourism, and beer tourism are all part of culinary tourism. It is more than just tasting and eating. It encompasses cooking schools, cookbook and kitchen gadgets stores, wine tasting tours, culinary tours, festivals and events, culinary media, guidebooks, caterers, wineries, breweries, distilleries, food growers and manufacturers, culinary attractions, and more.

Tasting delicious food is not only one of life's joys, but sometimes serves as a "window" to the history and culture of a remote area that you have never set foot on. Food, wine, and other culinary experiences are not only an important ingredient in travel but also a powerful motivation to travel. Travelers are stating that food is a key aspect of the travel experience and that they believe experiencing a country's food is essential to understand its culture.

Social media will become more critical to restaurant marketing. "Word of mouth" has moved online, and more consumers use the Web to browse menus, make reservations, and get recommendations from other diners.

Nowadays, ordering food through apps has become more commonplace than cooking in many households, as it is cheap, fast, and convenient. The majority of restaurants in the city, whether small establishments and street-food vendors, fancy restaurants, or fastfood chains, will surely be available to order through one or both of these apps.

Ordering food is as simple as opening the app, and scrolling through the dining choices near you. You will see an endless list of all the restaurants (usually within a 5-6 km radius) that are ready to take your order. If you want to narrow down your search, at the top of the page there will be categories of food to help focus your browsing, such as breakfast food, western food, fast food, etc.

If you have a specific food in mind, you can search for the food, and you will see dozens of results to choose from. Once you pick your restaurant of choice, you can scroll through the menu, which will always include pictures and prices, and simply select the food you want to order. If you are hesitant, each restaurant has its review page, where you can see customer's comments and pictures, so that you know exactly what you can expect to get.

## Ⅲ Situational Dialogue

### ➤ Dialogue 1

**Seating the Guests**

Scene: the hostess (A) of a restaurant is receiving a couple (B) without reservation.

A: Good evening, sir and madam. Welcome to our restaurant. Do you have a reservation?

B: I'm afraid not.

A: How many people are there in your party?

B: We would like a table for 4.

A: I'm afraid there is no table available right now. Would you mind waiting in the lounge for a few minutes?

B: How long do we need to wait?

A: I can seat you in 10 minutes. I will call you as soon as the table is ready.

(10 minutes later)

A: Sorry to have kept you waiting, sir and madam. You table is ready. This way, please.

B: Thank you.

A: A table for four, right? Would you like some drinks before your friends coming?

B: Ice water will be fine.

A: Just a moment, please.

(After a while, the hostess serves the ice water for them.)

A: Here is the menu, sir and madam. Take your time.

B: Thanks! We will be ready for order after our friends arrive.

A: OK, the waiter will come to take your order later.

### ➤ Dialogue 2

**At a Chinese Restaurant**

Scene: At a Chinese restaurant, a waiter (A) is taking orders for a couple (B).

A: Good evening, sir and madam, are you ready to order now?

B: Sorry, we have no idea for Chinese food. Could you give us some introduction?

A: I'm glad to. There are many different cuisine in China. Sichuan food is hot and spicy. Shanghai food is sweet. Cantonese food is light and fresh. What kind of flavor would you prefer, spicy or sweet, light or heavy?

B: I love spicy food, but my husband likes bland food.

A: How about Mapo tofu and steamed fish? They are our chef's specialty.

B: What's Mapo?

A: Mapo in Chinese is an old lady whose face is pockmarked. It is recorded that her tofu dishes are quite popular among the guests. However some guests told her that they want to eat some meat rather than just tofu. So she bought some beef and cut it to granules and adding the beef into her tofu. Then the tofu dish with beef become more popular and her guests gave the name Mapo tofu.

B: Sounds interesting. We will take them.

A: What vegetable dishes would you like?

B: What do you have?

A: Now is the season for spinach, would you like to try?

B: Well, How do you cook that?

A: Stir fry with garlic.

B: OK, we would like to have this. How about soup? Could you recommend us some soup?

A: I recommend one of our most popular soup—mushrooms with shrimp soup. It is very clear and fresh.

B: Sounds good. That will be all.

A: What would you like to have for staple, rice, noodle, or dumpling?

B: Steamed rice will be fine.

A: Would you like any drinks to go with your meal?

B: Do you have any local beer?

A: Liquan is our local brand. Would you like to try?

B: OK, one Liquan for me, please.

A: Well, May I repeat your order? Steamed fish, Mapo tofu, stir fry spinach with garlic, mushroom with shrimp soup, steamed rice and one Liquan beer.

B: Exactly!

A: Your meal should be out shortly. Would you like me to replace the chopsticks with knife and fork?

B: Thank you. You're very considerate!

A: Hope you have a nice evening.

## ➢ Dialogue 3

### Taking a la carte Order for Western Food

Scene: A couple comes to a Western food restaurant for dinner. The waiter (A) is taking order for the husband (B) and the wife (C) separately.

A: Good evening, sir and madam. Would you like to have table d'hote, or a la carte tonight?

B: A la carte, please. I'll have the shrimp cocktail to start.

A: What would you like for your main course?

B: I'd like the steak with potato.

A: How would you like your steak, rare, medium, or well-done?

B: Medium well with black pepper sauce, please.

A: What kind of potatoes would you like to go with that? Mashed, boiled or baked?

B: Mashed potatoes, please.

C: I would like to have scallop with a side salad.

A: Today we have garden salad, Caesar salad, and Greek salad. Which do you prefer?

C: I might go for the Caesar salad.

A: What dressing would you like to go with your salad? Oil with vinegar, Thousand Island sauce, or our house dressing?

B: I will try your house dressing.

A: Good. Would you care for soup to start with?

C: A cream and onion soup, please.

A: Anything for dessert?

B: I will skip the dessert today. Just give me a cup of black coffee.

C: I would like a strawberry jelly, please.

A: OK, one shrimp cocktail and medium well steak for gentleman, one cream and onion soup, scallop accompany with a Caesar salad and strawberry jelly for lady.

B: That's right. Thank you!

A: Your dishes will be coming soon. I am pleased at your service.

## ➢ Dialogue 4

### Serving Dishes

Scene: A couple (A) has been waiting for 20 minutes. They try to call the waiter's (B) attention.

A: Excuse me.

B: Yes, sir?

A: It has been 20 minutes since you took our order. How much longer do we have to wait for our dinner?

B: I am really sorry. I'll check your order with the chef right away.

(2 minutes later)

B: Sorry to have kept you waiting. Here is your mushroom with shrimp soup. It is very hot, please be careful. And this is the Liquan beer you ordered.

A: Could you bring us one more glass? My wife also wants to try some beer.

B: Sure. I will bring one to you immediately ... Here is your Mapo tofu and the glass you need. Please enjoy it.

A: Mm. It looks good. There are still two other dishes to be served, right?

B: They are coming. Shall I take the beer bottle away?

A: Yes, go ahead.

(30 minutes later)

B: This fruit platter is on the house. How do you like the food, sir and madam?

A: Yes, that was really a great meal. We both loved it.

B: I'm glad you liked it. Is there anything else I can get you?

A: No, thanks. That is quite enough. Be sure to give our compliments to the chef. The meal was fantastic.

B: I'll be sure to do that. Enjoy.

> **Dialogue 5**

### At the Bar

Scene: Bartender (A) is serving a guest (B) at the bar.

A: Good evening. What can I get for you?

B: What kinds of spirits do you have?

A: Quite a lot. Brandy, whisky, tequila, gin and rum ...

B: Scotch whisky, please.

A: How would you like your whisky, straight up or on the rocks?

B: On the rocks, please. Can I run a tab?

A: I'm afraid not. You'll have to pay as you go.

B: No problem. How much do I owe you?

A: $5 dollars, please. It's happy hour. All the drinks are half price until 8:00 p. m..

B: Great! And do you serve food here?

A: Only bar snacks. Would you like some chips to go with your drink?

B: That is a good idea!

## IV Chinese Stories

### Chinese Food Culture

Have you eaten yet? Don't be baffled by this question when a native Chinese says this to you or others at the first sight. It is just like the phrases: "How are you?" or "Good day" as a very common greeting in China. Similar to "Food is the staff of life"

in the West, the Chinese saying goes "To the people, food is heaven". Chinese people, at all levels of society, enjoy eating delicious food. The chefs were constantly challenged to create dishes with harmonious exciting combinations of flavors, textures and colors that centered on a love and respect for food.

The diversity of the country's climate, products and customs result in the widely different food styles and tastes in local regions. Colorful cooking methods and widely-used seasonings make rich flavors of Chinese dishes, and also result in the attractive look of the dishes, which comprises color, fragrance, taste, meaning form and nutrition. Chinese people use dozens of methods of cooking, like steaming, boiling, roasting, brewing, frying, braising, simmering, smoking and so on. Chinese dishes appeal to the senses through color, shape, aroma and taste. According to different regional styles, Chinese cuisine can be mainly divided into four kinds such as Sichuan, Cantonese, Shandong and Huaiyang, each is distinctly different. In addition to these traditional cuisine, the culinary industry in China has undergone great changes, as almost every place has its own local specialties and food styles, and the different cuisine gathered in big cities like Beijing and Shanghai.

**The Four Major Cuisines**

Shandong Cuisine tastes clean, pure and not greasy, is characterized by aroma, freshness, crispness and tenderness. Shallots and garlic are frequently used as main seasonings. Shandong chefs are good at cooking seafood such as sea cucumber, "squirrel fish", jumbo prawns, crab and eel. Classic dishes include steamed tofu, stuffed with vegetables, sea cucumber with scallion, shark's fin with three fillets, white steak with four treasures, yellow carp with sweet and sour sauce... Shandong cuisine leads the Northern dishes.

Cantonese cuisine tastes clean, light, crisp and fresh. Its basic techniques include steaming, braising, boiling or stir-frying. The main ingredients of this type of Chinese food are seafood, pork, chicken and vegetables, but could include almost anything. Ingredients are purchased and prepared the same day and cooked just before serving, using few spicy seasonings. In many seafood restaurants, diners can choose fish from the tanks in which they are swimming. It is a very healthy food since it uses minimum of oil. Famous Cantonese dishes include tender boiled chicken, roast goose, roast suckling pig, braised squab in brown sauce, honey roast pork, dim sum...

Huaiyang Cuisine, with a history of over 2000 years, is popular in the lower reaches of the Yangtze River. Its flavors are heavier and oilier than Cantonese cuisine, featuring preserved vegetables, pickles and salted meats. Huaiyang Cuisine tastes light, fresh and sweet. Fish and crustaceans are the main ingredients. Cooking techniques consist of stewing, braising, roasting, and simmering. Popular dishes include beggar's chicken, hairy crab, "eight treasure" duck, "drunken" chicken,

West Lake Fish, braised eel and yellow fish.

The typical Sichuan Cuisine tastes spicy. The zest of dishes is flavored with star anise, fennel seed, chili, coriander and other spices. Chili bean paste, peppercorns and garlic are also widely used. Chicken, pork, river fish and shellfish are popular ingredients. Many Sichuan dishes are prepared using chili oil, which gives a special taste to the food. Common cooking methods include smoking and simmering, which allow peppers and aromatic seasonings to infuse food with unforgettable tastes and aromas. Traditional dishes include the Gongbao (KungPao) chicken, shredded pork with garlic sauce, Mapo tofu, double-fried pork slices, hotpot.

China has local cuisines, imperial dishes, and dishes of ethnic minorities, such as Islamic dishes with a strong religious flavor and vegetarian dishes.

## Hot pot

In China, hot pot has a history over 1000 years and until now, it is still the most popular dish for social or family gathering. Hot pot seems to have originated in Mongolia where the main ingredient was meat, usually beef, mutton or horse. It then spread to southern China during the Tang Dynasty and was further established during the Mongolian Yuan Dynasty. By the Qing Dynasty, the hot pot became popular throughout China.

Chinese hot pot has its own flavor and design according to different area, which is also determined by different weather conditions. The most famous type is known as Chongqing hot pot, also known as Sichuan hot pot. It is featured by the herbs and spices used in the soup base. The next is the worldwide popular Mongolian hot pot in Northeast China Region. In north China, there is famous Beijing lamb hot pot also known as mutton hot pot. In south china such as Guangdong, people are more likely to have seafood hot pot and beef hot pot.

## Chinese Food Therapy

Chinese food therapy is a practice of healing using natural foods instead of medications. The practice is largely drawn from Traditional Chinese Medicine (TCM). One core principle of Chinese food therapy is that food shares the same origin as medicine and can be used, just like medicine, to treat diseases.

When Chinese started farming and agriculture over 4000 years ago, they began to understand that each plant has its own special effects on human body. However, proper documentation was only found around 500 B.C. The Yellow Emperor's Classic of Internal Medicine, which was written around 300 B.C., was most important in forming the basis of Chinese food therapy. It classified food by four food groups, five tastes and by their natures and characteristics. By continuously using foods on people and testing them by trial-and-error, Chinese were able to identify the nature, characteristics and functional effects of each food.

Chinese food therapy is under the guidance of TCM (Traditional Chinese Medicine) theory, by making use of food properties, taking appropriate cooking method to make into curative food, to regulate bodily function and get to health status or cure illnesses at early stage. It is based on the well-known fact that improper eating leads to illness and proper diet contributes to the body's health. The proper diet should combine the five tastes in good balance to promote internal body harmony.

The principle of Yin and Yang which governs TCM is also followed in Chinese food therapy. Practitioners believe that foods have different natural properties. TCM categorizes the nature of foods into five types: hot, warm, neutral, cool, and cold.

Hot and warm food like alcohol or spicy food nourishes Yang. Too much hot food in the body creates more heat in the body; and an excessive amount of heat in the body can cause physical symptoms like dry mouth, heartburn, oral ulcer, and constipation. On the opposite end of the spectrum are cooling foods, or food that nourishes the Yin in the body. Examples of cooling food include banana, cucumber and pear. Cooling food can be used to counter the excessive heat in the body, or reduce the excessive internal heat, and vice versa. Neutral food such as rice and black fungus is neither hot nor cool.

Principles of food therapy are as follows: Food treatment in accordance with local climate of different region; Food treatment in accordance with different people's body condition; Food treatment in accordance with seasonal conditions.

Each organ is paired with corresponding element and flavor. Spring is the season to nourish the liver. Foods such as chrysanthemum, goji-berry, sprout, dandelion and animal liver are all beneficial to our liver. Summer is the season to nourish the heart. Spicy hot and deep-fried foods should be restricted. Cooling foods such as watermelon, citrus fruits, turnips or mung beans, cucumber and bitter melon are more suitable. Autumn is the season to nourish the lung. Foods that can promote vital fluids are soy, spinach, asparagus, seaweed, pine nut, peanuts, pear, honey, sugar cane, oyster, and pork. Winter is the season to nourish the kidney. Plenty of warming yang foods and slightly fatty foods should be included in the diet. Examples of warming foods are ginger, cinnamon, chestnuts, onion, leek, chives, garlic, chicken, beef and lamb.

## Ⅴ Listening

**1. Listen to the conversation and fill in the blanks**

### Healthy Food

A: husband   B: wife

A: Darling, I got some _____!

B: Oh, I thought we said we would start our new healthy lifestyle. _____!

A: Right, so what did you get?

B: Well, healthy food, of course! I got some _____…

A: Organic? What's the difference between organic and regular food? Do we need organic carrots that are more expensive?

B: They _____. And yes, we need organic carrots.

A: Oh, so _____, right?

B: Yes, better for the environment and better for us!

A: But I really want some Coke.

B: Many people gain weight by drinking too much Coke. It _____ _____ and there's simply no nutritional value in it whatsoever. If you really want some Coke, _____.

A: It seems that I have no choice.

**2. Listen to the dialogue and judge true (T) or false (F) for each statement.**

### Serving Wrong Dishes

(1) Mrs. Jackson ordered a Garden salad. (    )

(2) Mrs. Jackson is allergic to cheese (    )

(3) The kitchen will take a quarter to make the duck breast. (    )

(4) The room service arranged at 9:00 p.m. is free. (    )

(5) Mr. Jackson doesn't take the sea bass. (    )

扫码
听听力

扫码
听听力

## Ⅵ Speaking

1. Discussion: Discuss the differences between Chinese food and Western food with your partner. Take notes and share with others in your own words.

| The differences between Chinese food and Western food | | |
|---|---|---|
| | Chinese food | Western food |
| Food material | | |
| Cooking method | | |
| Tastes | | |
| Nutrition | | |

2. Role play. Work in pairs and act out the following dialogues.

(1) At a local restaurant in Guilin, the waiter is introducing the local dishes for a foreign couple.

(2) A foreign couple is having dinner in a Chinese restaurant. They are vegetarian. The waitress is taking their order.

(3) Mr. Jackson is having dinner in a Chinese restaurant. He is interested in Chinese liquor. The waiter gives him an introduction and help him order some liquor.

## Ⅶ Writing

### Translation of Chinese Food

To translate Chinese menu into English, we must understand the composition and naming method of Chinese food. The name of Chinese food is usually composed of the name of ingredients, cooking method, color, flavor, shape, founder or birthplace of dishes. Due to the great difference between Chinese and English, we should try to translate the ingredients, cooking methods and flavors of dishes to make the guests clear at a glance.

**1. Translation beginning with main ingredient**

(1) Main ingredient(shape) ＋ with ＋ side ingredient

E. g.　　梅菜扣肉　　Pork with preserved vegetable

　　　　洋葱牛肉　　Beef with onion

(2) Main ingredient(shape) ＋with＋ flavor / juice

E. g.　　芥末鸭掌　　Duck webs with mustard sauce

　　　　咖喱鸡肉　　Chicken with curry

**2. Translation beginning with cooking method**

(1) Cooking method(ed) ＋ main ingredients (shape)

E. g.　　清蒸鱼　　　Steamed fish

　　　　烧鹅　　　　Roast goose

(2) Cooking method(ed) ＋ main ingredient (shape) ＋ with ＋ side ingredient

E. g.　　咸鱼蒸肉饼　Steamed pork cake with salted fish

　　　　土豆烧牛肉　Braised beef with potato

(3) Cooking method(ed) ＋ main ingredient (shape) ＋ with / in ＋ flavor / juice

E. g.　　红烧牛肉　　Braise beef with brown sauce

　　　　豉汁牛仔骨　Steamed beef ribs in black bean sauce

**3. Translation beginning with shape or taste**

(1) Shape / Taste ＋ main ingredient ＋ with ＋ side ingredient

E. g.　　芝麻酥鸡　　Crispy chicken with sesame

　　　　玉兔馒头　　Rabbit－shaped mantou

(2) Shape / Taste ＋ cooking method(ed) ＋ main ingredient

E. g.　　五香熏鱼　　Spiced smoked fish

　　　　琵琶大虾　　Pipa－shaped deep－fried prawns

(3) Shape / Taste ＋ main ingredient ＋ with / in ＋ flavor juice

E. g.　　白切鸡　　　Tender boiled chicken with soy sauce

　　　　豆瓣鱼　　　Spicy fish in black bean sauce

**4. Translation beginning with name of person or name of place**

(1) Name of person /place ＋ main ingredient

E. g.　　麻婆豆腐　　Mapo bean curd

　　　　东坡肉　　　Dongpo pork

(2) Name of person /place ＋ cooking method(ed) ＋ main ingredient

E. g.　　东坡煨肘　　Dongpo stewed pork joint
　　　　　北京烤鸭　　Beijing roast duck

**5. Freestyle translation**

Sometimes people choose a good and elegant name for dishes according to the characteristics of the main ingredients, color or the shape after cooking. For such artistic naming, the names of dishes are translated according to their ingredients and cooking methods. If "狮子头"is translated into lion head, it is easy for foreign diners to misunderstand.

E. g.　　生菜好市　　Lettuce with oyster sauce
　　　　　红烧狮子头　Braised pork balls with brown sauce

**1. Writing Skills**

### Menu

A restaurant menu is more than just a list of food with prices. It represents your restaurant concept. An effective menu can bring in new customers and keep them coming back.

Step 1

Choose menu items and create a list of appetizer, main course or cold dishes, meat dishes, vegetable dishes, soups, desserts and other items to include on the menu.

Step 2

Write a short description of each entree, appetizer and other items on the menu. Specific ingredients, method of preparation and visual descriptions are important.

Step 3

Design a menu layout that emphasizes the restaurant's theme. Choose appetizing colors, create categories for item placement and include a restaurant logo. Use a font that is easy to read. Place the price of each item next to the description and picture.

Step 4

Price items fairly and appropriately for the customer you serve. Take into consideration cost of food, cost of preparation, over head costs (rent, energy costs, health insurance for employees, etc.) and the average income of your customers.

Unit 5 Food and Beverage Service

2. Sample

**APPETIZERS**

| 01. | Vegetable Spring Roll (2) | 1.10 |
| 02. | Pork Egg Roll (1) | 1.20 |
| 03. | Shrimp Egg Roll (1) | 1.50 |
| 04. | Crab Rangoon (6) | 4.25 |
| 05. | Fried Chicken Wing (4) | 5.75 |
| 06. | Steamed Dumpling or Fried Pot Stickers (8) | 5.25 |
| 07. | Teriyaki Chicken | 5.25 |
| 08. | Barbecued Pork | 5.75 |
| 09. | Fried Wonton (12) | 3.15 |
| 10. | Sweet Donuts (10) | 3.25 |
| 11. | Fried Fish Fillet (4) | 5.25 |
| 12. | Combination Plate | 9.95 |

(2 egg rolls, 2 crab rangoons, 2 fried wontons, 2 teriyaki chickens, 2 fish fillets and 2 chicken wings.)

**SOUP**
(Served with crispy noodles)

| | | Pt. | Qt. |
|---|---|---|---|
| 20. | Wonton Soup | 1.75 | 3.15 |
| 21. | Egg Drop Soup | 1.75 | 3.15 |
| 22. | Chicken Noodle or Rice Soup | 1.75 | 3.15 |
| 23. | Wonton Mixed Egg Drop Soup | 1.95 | 3.75 |
| 24. | Hot & Sour Soup 🌶 | 1.95 | 3.75 |
| 25. | House Special Soup | --- | 4.25 |
| 26. | Vegetable Soup | --- | 3.75 |

**FRIED RICE**

| | | Sm. | Lg. |
|---|---|---|---|
| 30. | Chicken, Pork or Vegetable Fried Rice | 4.75 | 6.95 |
| 31. | Beef or Shrimp Fried Rice | 4.95 | 7.25 |
| 32. | House Fried Rice | 5.25 | 7.75 |

(Chicken, pork, and shrimp)

**LO MEIN**
(Soft Noodles)

| | | Sm. | Lg. |
|---|---|---|---|
| 35. | Chicken, Pork or Vegetable Lo Mein | 5.25 | 7.25 |
| 36. | Beef or Shrimp Lo Mein | 5.55 | 7.95 |
| 37. | House Lo Mein | 5.75 | 8.95 |

(Chicken, pork, and shrimp)

**CHOW MEIN OR CHOP SUEY**
(with Crispy Noodles) (Served with White Rice)

| | | Sm. | Lg. |
|---|---|---|---|
| 40. | Chicken, Pork or Vegetable | 5.25 | 7.25 |
| 41. | Beef or Shrimp | 5.25 | 7.25 |
| 42. | House | 5.75 | 8.25 |

(Chicken, pork, and shrimp)

🌶 Hot & Spicy
We can alter the spicy to your taste
Menu is subject to change

**CHICKEN**
(Served with white rice)

| | | Sm. | Lg. |
|---|---|---|---|
| 45. | Sweet & Sour Chicken | 5.25 | 7.75 |
| 46. | Chicken with Broccoli | 5.25 | 8.15 |
| 47. | Moo Goo Gai Pan | 5.25 | 8.15 |
| 48. | Chicken with Mixed Vegetables | 5.25 | 8.15 |
| 49. | Chicken with Snow Pea | 5.25 | 8.15 |
| 50. | Chicken with Mushroom | 5.25 | 8.15 |
| 51. | Chicken with Cashew Nut | 5.25 | 8.15 |
| 52. | Chicken with Garlic Sauce 🌶 | 5.25 | 8.15 |
| 53. | Curry Chicken | 5.25 | 8.15 |
| 54. | Kung Pao Chicken 🌶 | 5.25 | 8.15 |
| 55. | Chicken with Chinese Vegetables | 5.25 | 8.15 |
| 56. | Szechwan Chicken 🌶 | --- | 8.15 |
| 57. | Hunan Chicken 🌶 | --- | 8.15 |
| 58. | Black Pepper Chicken 🌶 | 5.25 | 8.15 |
| 59. | Almond Boneless Chicken (white meat) | 5.25 | 8.15 |

**PORK**
(Served with white rice)

| | | Sm. | Lg. |
|---|---|---|---|
| 60. | Sweet & Sour Pork | 5.25 | 7.75 |
| 61. | Pork with Broccoli | 5.25 | 8.15 |
| 62. | Pork with Mixed Vegetables | 5.25 | 8.15 |
| 63. | Pork with Garlic Sauce 🌶 | 5.25 | 8.15 |
| 64. | Hunan Pork 🌶 | 5.25 | 8.15 |

**BEEF**
(Served with white rice)

| | | Sm. | Lg. |
|---|---|---|---|
| 70. | Pepper Steak with Onions | 5.55 | 8.75 |
| 71. | Beef with Broccoli | 5.55 | 8.75 |
| 72. | Beef with Mixed Vegetables | 5.55 | 8.75 |
| 73. | Beef with Snow Pea | 5.55 | 8.75 |
| 74. | Beef with Mushroom | 5.55 | 8.75 |
| 75. | Beef with Garlic Sauce 🌶 | 5.55 | 8.75 |
| 76. | Curry Beef 🌶 | 5.55 | 8.75 |
| 77. | Szechwan Beef 🌶 | --- | 8.75 |
| 78. | Hunan Beef 🌶 | --- | 8.75 |
| 79. | Mongolian Beef 🌶 | --- | 8.75 |

**SHRIMP**
(Served with white rice)

| | | Sm. | Lg. |
|---|---|---|---|
| 80. | Sweet & Sour Shrimp | 5.95 | 8.25 |
| 81. | Shrimp with Broccoli | 5.95 | 9.15 |
| 82. | Shrimp with Snow Pea | 5.95 | 9.15 |
| 83. | Shrimp with Mixed Vegetables | 5.95 | 9.15 |
| 84. | Shrimp with Garlic Sauce 🌶 | 5.95 | 9.15 |
| 85. | Shrimp with Cashew Nut | 5.95 | 9.15 |
| 86. | Shrimp with Lobster Sauce | 5.95 | 9.15 |
| 87. | Hot Spicy Shrimp 🌶 | 5.95 | 9.15 |
| 88. | Kung Pao Shrimp 🌶 | 5.95 | 9.15 |
| 89. | Szechwan Shrimp 🌶 | 5.25 | 8.15 |
| 90. | Hunan Shrimp 🌶 | --- | 9.15 |

3. Writing Practice

Work in groups and design a menu for a new Chinese restaurant including starter, soup, meat dishes, vegetable dishes and staples.

# VIII Supplementary Reading

### "Clear your plate" Campaign

Food waste is a serious issue in China, especially in restaurants, because in Chinese culture it is the norm to order excess food to show generosity and respect to your guests. Food wasted by Chinese consumers each year is sufficient to feed millions of individuals for a year. "Clear your plate" campaign was launched in 2013 in an effort to reduce food waste. Many restaurants have adopted effective measures to stop food wastage and promote thrift, including providing assorted dishes or half-portion dishes at discounted prices, encouraging diners to order less and to take doggy bags.

### Vegetarian

Vegetarians and vegans don't eat products or by-products of slaughter. In most cases, vegetarians choose not to eat animals because they oppose treating them cruelly. They don't consume the flesh of any animal, including pigs, chickens, cows, sheep, and fish. They may also avoid foods that contain animal-derived ingredients such as gelatin (found in some sweets) and rennet (found in certain cheeses). In addition to avoiding all animal flesh, a strict vegetarian or vegans don't consume dairy products (such as milk, cheese, ice cream, and yogurt), eggs, or any other foods that are derived from animals.

| A vegetarian diet can include … | A vegetarian diet does not include … |
| --- | --- |
| Vegetables and fruits<br>Grains and pulses<br>Nuts and seeds<br>Eggs<br>Dairy products<br>Honey | Meat or poultry<br>Fish or seafood<br>Insects<br>Gelatin or animal rennet<br>Stock or fat from animals |

### The Michelin Star Restaurant

The Michelin Guide awards restaurants between one and three stars, and they are coveted. Getting one, or one more can create a legend; losing one can result in significant heartbreak. The Guide itself says that "certain establishments deserve to be brought to your attention" because of the quality of the cuisine served. Since the Michelin Guide started out as a guide to road-touring, the stars are not only associated with quality, but with driving value. The Michelin Guide uses a system of symbols to identify the best hotels and restaurants within each comfort and price category. For restaurants, Michelin stars are based on five criteria:

1. The quality of the products;
2. The mastery of flavor and cooking;
3. The "personality" of the cuisine;
4. The value for the money;
5. The consistency between visits.

3 stars mean the restaurant merits a special trip. The food, wine, decor and service will be exceptional and you should expect to pay and you should probably leave the kids at home.

2 stars indicate the restaurant deserves a detour. Everything will be top-notch, if not perfect, and you should not expect a bargain.

1 star means that if it's on your way, you should stop. For the kind of restaurant it is, a one star establishment should serve very good food in a pleasant environment. But, the Guide warns readers not to compare the very-fancy "deluxe" restaurant that has one star to a simpler restaurant where you can appreciate fine food at a reasonable price.

## Organic Food

Organic food is food grown without the use of pesticides, chemical fertilizers, hormones, or genetic modification. Organic food can refer to fruits and vegetables and also to meat, dairy products, eggs, and poultry.

There is widespread public belief that organic food is safer, more nutritious, and tastes better than conventional food. These beliefs have fueled increased demand for organic food despite higher prices. To be certified organic, products must be grown and manufactured in a manner that adheres to standards set by the country they are sold in.

## Junk food

Junk food is used to describe food that is high in fat, salt, or sugar but deficient in protein, fiber, minerals and vitamins, typically produced in the form of packaged snacks needing little or no preparation. Typical junk food include fried chicken, hamburger, potato chips / crisp. Pretzels, refined carbohydrates—e. g. candy, soft drinks, or saturated fats—e. g. cake, chocolate.

## British pub

"If you haven't been to a pub, you haven't been to Britain." Renowned the world over, the great British pub is not just a place to drink beer, wine, cider or even something a little bit stronger. They are places where people go to talk to each other, to find companionship, to gossip and catch up on news from near and far. Or play games like cards or darts or even billiards. The French have their cafés, Americans have their fast food, the English—and the British Isles in general—their pubs. Most pubs have no waiters—you have to go to the bar to buy drink. Pub culture is designed to promote sociability in a society known for its reserve. Standing at the bar for service allows you to chat with others waiting to be served. Sociological surveys have shown that the pub is the only place where the English willingly begin a conversation with a stranger!

## IX Check List

| Key Words | | | | |
|---|---|---|---|---|
| menu | cuisine | culinary | flavor | private room |
| banquet | buffet | gourmet | cafeteria | hot pot |
| cafe | canteen | vegetarian | recipe | house specialty |
| course | waiter | waitress | chef | main course |
| pastry | pasta | noodle | napkin | dairy product |
| tablecloth | chopsticks | knife | fork | platter |
| seasoning | condiment | ingredient | organic | side dish |
| sauce | vinegar | mustard | curry | oyster sauce |
| ketchup | soy sauce | honey | butter | french fries |
| jam | cream | sugar | pepper | take-out / away |
| appetizer | steak | salad | dessert | junk food |
| snack | dressing | yogurt | bar | mineral water |
| winery | brewery | distillery | pub | fish & chips |
| bartender | cocktail | liquor | spirits | vending machine |
| aperitif | liqueur | rum | gin | soda water |
| champagne | brandy | whisky | vodka | instant coffee |
| food court | food truck | food stall | bistro | combo meal |

## Useful Sentences

**Seating guests**

1. Good evening, ladies and gentlemen. Welcome to our restaurant.
2. Have you got a reservation, sir?
3. I'm sorry, we don't have any table available at the moment. Would you please wait a few minutes in the lounge over there? I will let you know as soon as the table is ready.
4. We can seat you very soon.
5. Now we have a table for you, would you please step this way?
6. Sorry to have kept you waiting. Now your table is ready.
7. I will show you to your table.
8. Is this table fine with you?
9. A table for eight, right?
10. The private room is upstairs.
11. Would you like a high chair for the baby?
12. Here's the menu. A waiter/waitress will come soon to take your order.
13. Take your time, please.

**Taking order**

1. Excuse me, sir. May I take your order now?
2. Would you like to have table d'hote or a la carte?
3. Would you like to order now?
4. Today's speciaty is ... Would you like to try?
5. Which flavor would you prefer, sweet or chili?
6. Maybe Cantonese cuisine will suit you.
7. Would you like to try our house specialty?
8. It is a local specialty.
9. What would you like for the cold dishes?
10. What vegetable dishes would you have?
11. We had a wide range of vegetarian dishes for you to choose from.
12. It's crisp/tasty/ tender/ clear/ strong/ spicy/ aromatic.
13. It looks good, smells good and tastes good.
14. It's for 4 persons.
15. It's out of season.
16. Why not try our buffet dinner?
17. It is our chef's recommendation.
18. If you are in a hurry, I would recommend ...
19. What would you like for the appetizer / main course / dessert?
20. How would you like your steak, rare, medium or well done?
21. What kind of salad do you prefer?
22. What kind of dressing would you like on your salad?
23. Your food will be ready soon. Please wait a moment.

**Serving dishes**

1. May I serve dishes now or later?
2. Here is the fried beef with green pepper and onion.
3. This is very hot. Please be careful.
4. This food is best eaten while hot. The dish loses its flavor when it gets cold.
5. Please enjoy it.
6. Excuse me, sir. May I separate the dish for everyone?
7. There is still some soup left. Would anyone care for some?
8. May I bring you a knife and a fork? It seems you are not used to chopsticks.
9. Excuse me, sir. May I change the plate for you?
10. May I move this plate to the side?
11. Shall I change this plate with a smaller one?
12. May I take the glass away?
13. May I clear the table for you?

**Handling problems**

1. I do apologize for giving you the wrong dish.
2. I'll change it immediately for you.
3. They're on the house.
4. We will serve you another course for free.
5. I assure you it won't happen again.
6. I'm sorry to hear that. That's unusual. I'll look into the matter at once.
7. The money for the meal is half, madam.

**Bar service**

1. Good afternoon/evening, welcome to the bar.
2. What would you like to drink?
3. How would you like your whisky, straight up or on the rocks, sir?
4. It's happy hour. All the drinks are half price until 8:00 p.m..
5. Here is your beer/drink, sir.
6. I'll bring you some crisps and peanuts.
7. Enjoy yourself.

# Unit 6
# Tourist Destination

**Learning Objectives**

After learning this part, you should be able to:
1. understand the nature and roles of destination in the wider tourism industry.
2. understand the role of DMO and information center.
3. develop a scientific outlook on development by learing to describe a destination about its history, geography, natural environment, and social development.

## I. Lead In

Put the following countries in the correct continent.

| | | | | |
|---|---|---|---|---|
| Japan | Egypt | Singapore | Canada | South Korea |
| Italy | Spain | Mexico | Russia | the United States |
| Germany | Turkey | Malaysia | France | United Kingdom |
| Australia | Portugal | Chile | Thailand | New Zealand |
| Brazil | Indonesia | Argentina | Switzerland | the Philippines |

| Asia | Europe | North America | South America | Oceania | Africa |
|---|---|---|---|---|---|
| | | | | | |

## 📖 Background Reading

### Tourist Destination

The destination sits at the core of the wider tourism system in that it represents an amalgam of tourism products that collectively offer a destination "experience" to visitors. For many consumers (day visitors and tourists), particularly in leisure tourism, the destination is the principal motivating factor behind the consumer's decision and expectations.

There is currently no widely accepted definition of the term **tourist destination**. From the tourism industry supply perspective, a destination is usually defined by a geo-political boundary, given destination marketing is most commonly funded by governments. From the traveler perspective, a destination might be perceived quite differently. Tourists' expectations when visiting a particular place are related to several features of the chosen destination: culture, architecture, gastronomy, infrastructure, landscape, events, shopping, etc. These features attract people to the destination and contribute to the overall experience of the trip.

Destinations come in all shapes and sizes and can be found in a variety of geographic settings such as an urban, rural and coastal environment. Destinations can be countries and a collection of countries, a distinct state, county or province, or in fact represent a local city, town or resort, national park, area of outstanding natural beauty or coastline. France, the United States, and Spain were the three most popular international destinations in 2019. The total number of international travelers arriving in those countries was over 252 million. Although some years back, Africa was lean on tourism, the continent is currently regarded as the second fastest growing tourism region with over 67 million tourists in 2018. Ethiopia with a growth rate of 48.6% in 2018 is at the top of the list of African tourist centers.

There are many types of destinations that can be identified, but the most basic classification is threefold:

(1) Coastal destinations, epitomized in the ever-popular seaside resort that has undergone many changes since its modern-day emergence in the mid eighteenth century with advocacy of inland spas and sea bathing for health cures. A beach is always an excellent location for a relaxing holiday. With vast stretches of white sand, clear turquoise waters, waving palm trees, and a tranquil ambiance, vacationing at the beach is always as fun as it sounds. Whether you love relaxing on the sand, snorkeling in clear warm waters, or try the athlete in yourself with exciting water sports, a beach always offers an activity to suit everyone.

(2) Urban/city destinations offer a broad and heterogeneous range of cultural, architectural, technological, social and natural experiences and products for leisure and business. City destination is often the tourism gateways to their surrounding region. Locations that associate themselves with a major city destination may benefit from the latter's high volumes of visitors. The top urban destinations in the world include Hong Kong, London, New York, Paris, Shanghai and many other famous metropolis.

(3) Rural destinations that range from the ordinary countryside to national park, wilderness areas, mountains and lakes. The visitor's experience is related to a wide range of products generally linked to nature-based activities, agriculture, rural lifestyle or culture, angling and sightseeing.

Access is a key factor in determining the development of tourism and this can be clearly seen with the development of transport infrastructure and services that have heralded the development and spread of tourism nationally and internationally. **Economic distance** becomes an important factor in determining which locations or destinations are within the scope of a potential tourist region (Economic distance in this sense is the geographical distance, taking into account the cost of travel in terms of actual costs and time).

## Destination Management Organization (DMO)

Destination management refers to a broad management process and a holistic approach, where many aspects of a destination are managed via a coordinated process. It can include managing marketing, local accommodation, tours, events, activities, attractions and transportation, and is often the responsibility of a dedicated destination management organization, or DMO for short.

DMO is an organization that is normally under the jurisdiction of the local, regional or national government and has political and legislative power as well as the financial means to manage the destination's resources rationally and to ensure that all stakeholders can benefit in the long term.

From a traditionally marketing and promotion, focus the trend is to become leading organizations with a broader mandate which includes strategic planning, coordination and management of activities within an adequate governance structure with the integration of different stakeholders operating in the destination under a common goal. DMO helps to establish a competitive edge for the destination, ensure long-term sustainability, strengthen institutional governance, and build a strong and vibrant brand identity around your destination.

A DMO may use a wide range of marketing techniques, including display advertising, content marketing, social media promotion, offline advertising and experiential marketing. Destination marketing forms a key part of wider DMO responsibilities, helping to make a destination stand out from alternatives and hold a unique appeal for potential travelers.

**Tourist information center**

When planning tourist destination, it is often desirable to establish a tourist center that acts as the hub and gateway to various parts of the area, sometimes referred to as a "welcome center" that provided a one-stop, physical location from which travelers can connect to local businesses and services. It is an office that supplies information to people who are visiting an area for pleasure or interest, for example advice on things to see, accommodation, maps and restaurants, etc. They are operated at the airport, railway station or other port of entry.

These centers provide a welcoming environment for travelers to congregate, learn about available tourism products and services in the region, and make reservations. In addition, tourism information centers can provide a space to generate revenue through the sale of merchandise and local handicrafts as well as capture and analyze important traveler information and statistics. Visitor centers not only provide information and reservation services to travelers, but also service local tourism suppliers and the greater community.

**Tourism Area Life Cycle**

Butler's Tourism Area Life Cycle Model provides a fundamental underpinning to travel and tourism management of destinations. Butler's model is a line graph that shows the different stages in tourism development over time.

(1) Exploration—The exploration stage marks the beginning. A small number of tourists visit the area. The area is unspoilt and few tourist facilities exist. Inconvenient transport and lack of facilities restrict the number of visitors and influence its development. The nature and social economic environment of the destination has not changed because of tourism.

(2) Involvement—The involvement stage marks the beginning of tourism development. Guesthouses may start to open. Foreign investors may start to show an interest in development. Governments may be under pressure to develop transport infrastructure and community resources, such as airports, road layouts and healthcare provision. The involvement stage may mark the emergence of seasonality in tourism. Local communities actively provide services for visitors and take part in planning, developing and advertising the resort to attract an increased and regular number of visitors.

(3) Development—During the development stage, there will be lots of building and planning. New roads, train stations and airports may be built. New tourist attractions may emerge. Hotels and hospitality provisions will be put in place. During

the development phase, there will likely be an increase in marketing and promotion of the destination. There could be increased media and social media coverage.

During this time, the tourist population may begin to out-number the local population. Local control becomes less common and top-down processes and international organizations begin to play a key role in the management of tourism. The area becomes recognized as a tourist destination.

(1) Consolidation—During the consolidation stage, tourism growth slows. This may be intentional, to limit tourist numbers or to keep tourism products and services exclusive, or it may be unintentional. There will generally be a close tie between the destination's economy and the tourism industry. In some cases, destinations have come to rely on tourism as a dominant or their main source of income.

Many international chains and conglomerates will likely be represented in the tourism area. This represents globalization and can have a negative impact on the economy of the destination as a result of economic leakage. It is during this stage that discontent from the local people may become evident. Some tensions develop between the host and the tourists. This is one of the negative social impacts of tourism.

(2) Stagnation—The stagnation stage represents the beginning of a decline in tourism. During this time, visitor numbers may have reached their peak and the **tour environment capacity** reaches or exceeds the biggest limit already. The destination may simply be no longer desirable or fashionable. Tourism causes many economical social and the environmental problems. The destination is perceived to be "out of fashion".

(3) Decline or rejuvenation—The final stage of Butler's Tourism Area Life Cycle Model represents a range of possible outcomes for the destinations along the spectrum between rejuvenation and decline. The outcome of this will depend upon the plans and actions of the stakeholders of the said tourism development project.

Rejuvenation can occur through major redevelopment. Investment and modernization may occur which leads to improvements of facilities and introduction of new attractions, sustainable tourism approaches are adopted or there is a change in the target market.

If changes do not occur, there may be a slow continuation of tourism decline. Repeat clients are no longer satisfied with the available product. No attempt is made by destination stakeholders to revitalize the local tourist product, or these attempts are unsuccessful. New competitors emerge to divert and capture traditional market sources. People lose their jobs related to tourism. The image of the area suffers and a heavy decrease in their share of the market.

The destination life cycle should not be regarded as an unavoidable process, but rather one that can be re-directed through appropriate management measures to realize the outcomes that are desired by destination stakeholders.

## Situational Dialogue

### ➤ Dialogue 1

Dream Destination

Scene：Rick（A）is talking about his dream destination with his girlfriend Lily（B）

A：I'm going to have a three-week vacation. How about planning a trip?

B：Really? You've been dreaming of going to the United States for years. Now it's on the agenda.

A：Sounds exciting. I want to visit the Grand Canyon.

B：Good idea. And we can stay a couple of days in Las Vegas and have some fun in those casino hotels.

A：To understand America is to travel its highways. How about driving along California coastal line highway 1 from San Francisco to Los Angeles.

B：Wow, that is the road trip of a lifetime.

A：And the New York City can't be missed out. I'd like to watch a Broadway play.

B：But it's on the other side of the county and we have to fly five hours to get there.

A：It doesn't matter.

B：Then I can stroll in the central park and do a lot of shopping on Fifth Avenue. How exciting!

A：Wake up and smell the coffee! We don't have budget for luxury shopping.

B：Anyway, with so many places to visit and things to do, we really need to make a good plan.

A：I can't wait anymore.

### ➤ Dialogue 2

At the Tourist Information Center

Scene：Wang Xiao(A) is a staff working in the tourist information center. He is receiving a guest (B) inquiry.

A：Good morning, may I help you?

B：Good morning, do you have any free map of the city?

A：Yes, we do. And we also have a free information booklet.

B: Great. Could we have one please?

A: Sure, here you go.

B: Thank you. That's very nice of you.

A: You are welcome. Is there anything special you want to see?

B: We're here only for one day. Which places are the most-sees?

A: Guilin is a small city and most of parks, hills and historic sites are located in the center of the city within easy walking distance. Let me show you on the map. This is where we are, When you go out, just turn left and walk around the "Two Rivers and Four Lakes" area which is a perfect combination of natural scenery and historical culture. The landmark of Guilin, Elephant Trunk Hill, is at the other end of this area.

B: I heard that Guilin played an important role during the anti-Japanese period. Are there any historic sites we can visit today?

A: Guilin Office of the Eighth Route Army is open to the public without admission charges.

B: When does the museum close?

A: It is open until 4:00 p.m..

B: Do you think I can walk there?

A: You'd better take a taxi. It is about 3 kilometers from the Elephant Trunk Hill Park. Or you can take Bus No. 2.

B: By the way, do you have the sightseeing bus hop-on hop-off?

A: Yes. You can appreciate the amazing night view around the city if you take the night view sightseeing bus.

B: That's fantastic! Thank you very much!

A: It's my pleasure! Enjoy your stay in Guilin.

## ➢ Dialogue 3

### Yangshuo, a Global Village

Scene: Wang Lei(B) is a student of Guilin Tourism University. He met a foreign student (A) in the campus. They are talking about Yangshuo.

A: Hi, Wang Lei, I watched a very interesting video yesterday. An Chinese old lady gave directions to two foreign young men in fluent English.

B: Don't be surprised! The video was shot in Yangshuo, a town which enjoys the best scenery in Guilin. Besides the local accent of Yangshuo, English has become the language for daily use.

A: Really? Why is English so popular in Yangshuo?

B: Yangshuo is one of the first places in China to open to the world. In the past 40 years, so many foreigners settle down there after their visit and open restaurants and coffee shops, enjoy the easy life and outdoor sports. West street, the oldest street in Yangshuo, is called "the foreigner street". You can not only find Chinese teahouses, antiques, calligraphy, paintings, arts and crafts and try different Western-style cuisine in numerous foreign restaurants, hotels and pubs, but also see old Chinese ladies bargain with foreign tourists in English and foreigners chatting with local people in fluent Chinese.

A: What an amazing scene! It is a blend of Chinese and Western cultures. I am thinking about spending this weekend there, is it far from here?

B: It is 66 kilometers to the south of Guilin, buses run from Guilin Bus Station to Yangshuo every 20 minutes from 7:00 a.m. to 8:00 p.m..

A: Is there anything I can't miss when I'm in Yangshuo?

B: Bamboo rafting is one of the most popular activities in Yangshuo. Lean back and relax in a comfortable chair on a bamboo raft, floating slowly down the peaceful and clean waters of Yulong River, where you will see farmers working in picturesque rice paddies, water buffaloes and cows, ducks paddling on the water, and the reflection of the mountains in the clear water.

A: What a peaceful picture!

B: Along the Yulong River are many trails great for either cycling or hiking. Cycling along the country roads will take you through many local villages, bringing you in close contact with local people and allowing you to gain insight into their lives.

A: It is a perfect place for me to see rural China and the lifestyle of local people.

B: Yangshuo is also a world-famous site for rock climbing. Due to the advantageous Karst geography conditions, Yangshuo provides people with ideals to climb rock. A number of rock climbing operators offer more than 200 available routes locally. Whether you are a beginner or an expert climber, you'll find adventure in Yangshuo!

A: Wow, sounds like a lot of fun. How about food and night life?

B: There's a really good night life there, you can hang out in pubs with live music along the West street and try the local beer fish or Western-style cuisine.

A: Wow! I really look forward to the weekend. Thank you so much for telling me so much about Yangshuo.

B: You're welcome. You'll love it there.

## ➢ Dialogue 4

### City Pass

Scene: Jack (A) is going to visit Shanghai. Chloe (B), his friend, is giving him some information.

A: I am going to spend a week in Shanghai to explore this metropolis. The admission ticket will cost me a fortune.

B: Why don't you try city pass?

A: What is city pass?

B: City pass is a pre-paid ticket booklet with admission tickets to a handful of the most popular tourist destinations in major cities. It offers admission at around half off the price if tickets were purchased separately. With Shanghai city pass, you can choose attractions from 18 of Shanghai's greatest attractions, including Oriental Pearl Tower, Huangpu River Cruise, and more.

A: That will save me a lot of money!

B: You can skip long lines and enjoy the privileged access to the most popular attractions by scanning the same QR code at each different attraction.

A: That will save a lot of time for sightseeing. How long is the city pass valid for?

B: It is valid for 365 days after your purchase and is automatically activated after its first use and will then be active for 7 days, which is measured in 24-hour blocks.

A: It is reasonable!

B: You can also enjoy unlimited free travel on Shanghai City Sightseeing Tour Bus and some discount when shopping or having dinner in designated stores or restaurants.

A: What a brilliant product! How much is it?

B: The price ranges from 275 to 439 yuan. There are six different plans for people with different preference.

A: I'll look into it and find the best plan for myself. Thank you for your sharing.

B: You're welcome.

## IV Chinese Stories

### Guilin, an International Destination

"East or west, Guilin landscape is best!" Located in the northeast of Guangxi Zhuang Autonomous Region in south China, Guilin, which means "Forest of osmanthus", a type of evergreen bush with strong fragrant flowers in autumn, is considered to be the pearl of China's thriving tourist industry on account of the natural beauty and historic treasures. Covering an area of about 27800 square kilometers, the city is rather compact when compared with other leading cities in the country. With its mild subtropical climate, it is a pleasant place to visit Guilin at any time of the year. Generally April to September is considered to be the best time to visit Guilin. The most attractive and highlights of Guilin can be perfectly presented to people from all over the world during this period.

Guilin is also an important cultural city with a history of more than 2000 years. According to the recorded history, the First Emperor Qin Shihuang launched his ambitious campaign to conquer the south China and built the oldest contour canal in the world (in 214 B.C.) called Ling Canal in the north of Guilin. After he united the whole country, a prefecture was set up to administrate the area. The city has been the political, economic and cultural center of Guangxi since the Northern Song Dynasty.

Guilin is a multi-ethnic area with a population of 5.4 million, Han, Zhuang, Miao, Yao, Dong, Hui, Jing, Yi, Shui, Man and other ethnic groups live in harmony in the city. The regional ethnic culture with multi-ethnic integration constitutes an important feature of Guilin's urban culture. Simple folk customs and unique regional cultures including farming, festivals, costumes, eating and drinking, weddings and funerals, architecture, language and religious beliefs make up Guilin's rich and colorful folk customs.

Sitting on the Li River surrounded by dramatic limestone hills known as karst formations, Guilin attracts tens of thousands tourists from home and abroad every year. The landscape is decorated with lofty peaks, steep cliffs, fantastic caves, farming villages, and bamboo groves. With its breathtaking scenery and the tranquil life far away from the concrete metropolis, the scenic area is one of the top tourist attractions in China. Major attractions include Elephant Trunk Hill, Li River, Reed Flute Cave and Seven-Star Park.

## Elephant Trunk Hill

Elephant Trunk Hill is the symbol and unmistakable landmark of Guilin City that stands downtown on the conjunction of the Li River and the Peach Blossom River, which enjoys a very special appearance. The whole hill looks exactly like a huge elephant stretching its trunk drinking water of the Li River, hence the name. It is the masterpiece of karst landscape, composed of pure limestone deposited on seabed 360 million years ago. Between the "trunk" and the "body" is a vast round cave which resembles a full moon on water, hence the name Moon-over-Water Cave. When the waters wave and the moonlight gleams, the scene is exceedingly enchanting.

## Li River Cruise

The 83-kilometer-long waterway from Guilin to Yangshuo is the masterpiece of Li River. Along the river, the rolling peaks, steep cliffs, green hills and clear water constitute a fascinating hundred-mile pictures gallery. Taking a leisurely cruise to Yangshuo along the Li River is a perfect way to enjoy the natural scenery of the area. Nowadays bamboo rafting on the river is also available, which runs between Yangdi and Nine Horses Fresco Hill near Xingping. It is said to be the most impressive part along the river.

## Reed Flute Cave

Reed Flute Cave got its name from the verdant reeds growing outside it, with which people make flutes. Actually, inside this water-eroded cave is a spectacular world of various stalactites, stone pillars and rock formations created by carbonate deposition. Illuminated by colored lighting, the fantastic spectacle is found in many variations. Walking through the serried stone pillars, tourists feast their eyes on changing spots, feeling they are in a paradise where the Gods live. Top spot inside Reed Flute Cave is the Crystal Palace which is the widest part inside Reed Flute Cave. This is a brilliant hall and the height decreases to all sides. The stalactites are hanging up in four directions, and they are like series lanterns decorating the hall. Under the light effects, some stalagmites look like jumping fish.

## Seven Star Park

Seven Star Park, covering an area of more than 120 hectares, is the largest comprehensive park with mass scenery in Guilin City. It was so named because of the seven peaks, the four peaks of Putuo Mountain and three of Crescent Hill, inside resemble the form of the Big Dipper constellation. The Seven Star Park is endowed with elegant mountains, clear water, miraculous stone forest, deep and serene valleys, plentiful animals and plants and valued cultural relics. The main sights contain Flower Bridge, Putuo Mountain, Seven Star Cave, Camel Hill, Crescent Hill, Guihai Forest of Stele and Light of China Square.

## Two Rivers and Four Lakes

Scattered around the downtown Guilin, the four lakes—Gui, Rong, Shan and Mulong are like four pieces of green jade which connect Li River in the east and Peach Blossom River in the west. They together basically restored the round-the-city waterway attraction which got started in the Song Dynasty (960-1279 A.D.).

The crystal clear water gleams under the blue sky, swans wander in the water, egrets hover over the lake. With its breathtaking scenery and taste of a life escaping from the bustling city, the water system cruise has become one of Guilin's top tourist attractions. A 1.5 hours cruise offers a chance to view Guilin's tranquil mountain and water scenery, along with traditional Chinese architecture, ancient inscriptions on the bridge arches and well-maintained park-style lake frontage, from the best vantage point: on the water itself.

Guilin also has the ruins of the Zengpiyan Cave, the Ling Canal, Jingjiang Princes' Palace and Tomb, the Gongcheng Confucius Temple, the Eighth Route Army Office, the former residence of Li Zongren and other cultural relics of great historical, literary, and artistic value.

There are some well-preserved ancient towns and villages in Guilin area, such as Daxu old town, Xiong Village, Jiangtouzhou Village, etc. In these places, you will still catch a glimpse of old way of life and aged architecture, and can even sit down and chat with some of them at their home.

Compared with Beijing, Xi'an and Shanghai, Guilin is a lovely smaller town, which is an ideal place for international travelers to have a break and relax, especially after a long trip in China. Thanks to its natural beauty and slower life pace, Guilin is one of the best destinations for hiking and cycling in this country. Cycling leisurely on country roads, you will have a great opportunity not only to get closer to nature, but also to know more about the real life in South China's countryside. Even to have a walk around the lakes at city downtown is also pleasant and rewarding.

The local cuisine of Guilin reflects the features of combination of Hunan (spicy) and Guangdong (fresh, tender and light) cuisines due to the strategic locations between the 2 provinces. There are also many well-known snacks in the area: rice noodle, mugwort sticky rice cake, hammered tea cooked with oil, sticky rice balls, steamed muffin and braised water snails, etc. Rice noodle is a must-try—rice noodles in a broth of pork, beef, sour bamboo shoots, sour cowpea, and crisp soybean. The delicacy is served on every street corner in Guilin, and customers are expected to add the seasoning ingredients themselves.

The Sanhua alcohol, fermented bean curd and chili sauce are considered to be the city's three treasures, and are top choices among travelers. Products made from sweet-scented osmanthus are also recommended since the name of Guilin literally means forests of osmanthus. Osamnthus tea, sugar and wine will bring you sweet memories of this city.

Guilin has been opened to the outside world in early 1970s. Being one of most popular destinations for tourists in China, Guilin is a well-developed tourist center with convenient transportation, communication and accommodation facilities. You can enter Guilin by air, by train or by bus and get around on free buses. From luxury hotels to hostels, from splendid restaurants to local snacks, you are sure to find that your needs will be met beyond your expectations.

## V Listening

**1. Listen to the dialogue and fill in the blanks.**

**Introducing Destination**

A: Hi, Jane. I _____. Can you tell me a place interesting to visit?

B: What about Guilin?

A: Oh. It is supposed to be very beautiful.

B: You're right. I stayed there for a whole week, I'd have _____ _____.

A: Really? Would you tell me something about it?

B: With pleasure. Guilin _____. It's world famous for its oddly-shaped solitary hills rising out of flat ground in various shapes. Some _____ _____ etc.

A: Could you tell me some of the famous hills there?

B: They are Solitary Beauty Peak, Folded Brocade Hill, Ripple Hill, and Elephant Trunk Hill. Many hills have their stories. Among these hills, Solitary Beauty Peak may be _____. Climbing to the top of it you _____ of the city, the Li River and surrounding hills.

A: I hear that the caves are also as well known as the hills, aren't they?

B: Yes. Almost every hill has at least one cave. The best knowns are _____ _____.

A: I hear that Guilin is not only famous for its good view of the hills, but also for its good view of the Li River.

B: You're right. _____, and no matter how deep the water is you can see the bottom—_____.

A: Did you _____?

B: A visit to Guilin would not be complete _____ _____ to Yangshuo. This scenery of Li River is called "natural arts gallery" since a natural scenic wonder unfolds on both banks of the river. A trip ending in the hills around Yangshuo will inspire the phrase "_____ _____."

A: You really had a wonderful trip. I'd definitely go to Guilin for a visit.

**2. Listen to the dialogue and judge true (T) or false (F) for each statement.**

**Sanya, China's Hawaii**

1. Beaches, diving and sea wind are the three eternal themes in Sanya. (　)

2. Sanya's winter is warm with a temperature of 24℃. (　)

3. The experience in Sanya is fantastic but expensive. (　)

4. Fantasy Town in Haitang Bay is good for water sports fans. (　)

5. Yalong Bay is the best bay in the city. (　)

6. Sanya is a good destination for shopping because there are some duty-free stores there. (　)

## Ⅵ Speaking

**1. Discussion**: Discuss the differences among different destinations with your partner. Take notes and share with others in your own words.

| Comparison of different kinds of destinations | | | |
|---|---|---|---|
| Types of destination | Main attractions | Amenities | Activities |
| Coastal destination | | | |
| Urban destination | | | |
| Rural destination | | | |

**2. Role play**: Work in pairs and act out the following dialogues.

(1) Xiao Jin is a staff working at the visitor center. A guest is inquiring about tourist attractions around Guilin. Xiao gives introductions and answers the guest's question.

(2) Jack's dream destination is Japan. He is talking with a friend and planning a tour to Japan.

(3) Sam wants to know about the night life in Guilin. Lily gives her introductions.

## Ⅶ Writing

**1. Writing skills**

### Tourist Ads

Advertising is a very important promotional tool used in tourism marketing campaign because its influence is achieved by through the use of press, television, magazines, Internet, social media and other mass media. The ultimate purpose of ads is to appeal and stimulate travel desire and needs by designing some creative and attractive visual image, words or symbols.

The layout of a written advertisement usually consists of four parts:

(1) a very striking headline which will catch the client's eye and to read the followings;

(2) brief but persuasive body with necessary details.

(3) clear signature or easily identified logo, with address and contact manner.

(4) some impressive pictures of illustrations.

## 2. Sample

### Timeless Memories

Enjoy the best of what Maldives has to offer—a tropical paradise where time stands still. Beautifully appointed beach, villa along stretches of soft coral sand or above water bungalows as your vacation heavens. Wake up in paradise to the sound of the sea, dive amidst exotic underwater marvels and dine under a majestic star-studded sky over one of the finest Maldives luxury resorts.

Play hard—Go on excursions and day cruise to discover the coast in a catamaran. Go big game fishing or visit the local fishing village. Or do Nothing—Bask in the tropical sun or pamper yourself at our health spa, indulge in our unique cuisine—a delightful blend of Mediterranean and oriental tastes.

## 3. Writing Practice

You are supposed to write an advertisement for a tourist destination / hotel / scenic spot.

# VIII Supplementary Reading

## Accessible Tourism

According to the World Health Organization (WHO), 15% of the world's population (1 billion people) is estimated to live with some form of disability. UNWTO is convinced that accessibility for all to tourist facilities, products, and services should be a central part of any responsible and sustainable tourist policy. Accessible tourism is tourism and travel that is accessible to all people, with disabilities or not, including those with mobility, hearing, sight, cognitive, or intellectual and psycho-social disabilities, older persons and those with temporary disabilities. Accessible tourism enables people with access requirements, including mobility, vision, hearing and cognitive dimensions of access, to function independently and with equity and dignity through the delivery of universally designed tourism products, services and environments. This definition is inclusive of all people including those travelling with children in prams, people with disabilities and seniors. Accessible tourism provides opportunities for all types of people to take part in tourism activities.

## Special Interest Tourism

Special interest tourism is the provision of customized tourism activities that caters to the specific interests of groups and individuals. Special interest tourism can be categorized based on the type of interest that motivates people to travel, for example, adventure tourism, in which tourists look for thrilling activities and extreme sports, such as mountaineering, rafting, trekking, bungee jumping, scuba diving, paragliding, rock climbing and so on; sports tourism, in which tourists can either travel to another place in order to participate in a sport, or just to watch it being played; wellness tourism, which refers to traveling for the purpose of maintaining and enhancing one's body, mind, and soul with the use of massages, body treatments or meditation.

## Staycation

More and more people are starting to take a "staycation". That is, instead of traveling, many people are opting to stay at home and enjoy local recreational activities. With the economic climate and the desire to reduce the carbon footprint, Staycations have achieved high popularity in the financial crisis of 2007-2009 in which unemployment levels and gas prices are high.

A staycation (or stay-cation, or stacation) is a neologism for a period of time in which an individual or family stays at home and relaxes at home or takes day trips from their home to area attractions. Common activities of a staycation include use of the backyard pool, visits to local parks and museums, and attendance at local festivals. Some staycationers also like to follow a set of rules, such as setting a start and end date, planning ahead, and avoiding routine, with the goal of creating the feel of a traditional vacation. Some use their staycation as therapy—relaxing around the house or futzing in the garden—while others may use the time for projects or home repairs.

## Couch-surfing

Couch-surfing is a new way of traveling which travelers stay overnight with a series of hosts who typically provide basic accommodations (such as a couch to sleep on or a spare room) at no cost while traveling. Except from saving money, couch-surfer is being able to get an authentic experience of their host country, a true life, up close and personally look at different cultures, families, and households.

Couch-surfing hosts in theory, are sociable, interesting people who will broaden your horizons and your social circle by introducing you to so many more people—like their friends and family. And it will give you an unparalleled opportunity to learn about the people, the culture, the traditions, local places of interest to visit and listen to tales about the history, romance, local folklore and legends surrounding the area you are visiting. Your host family will be able to take you to all the awesome local hangouts, the best restaurants, the most vibey pubs, show you around and give you an opportunity to experience life as a local by visiting places that won't have made it to your tourist guide book.

You will have to have an open mind as you are a guest in a stranger's home and not everything will be to your liking and their way of life may be completely different from yours, so you will need to really decide before hand if you will be able to deal with the culture shock, or if it will be something you will embrace. Under their roof you are going to have to abide by their rules and regulations. You may be lucky to get the best accommodation, awesome hosts who hand you a key and tell you to make yourself at home and come and go as you please, or you might get those who want you to only use certain rooms of the house and to be in by a certain time at night.

**Gexu of the Zhuang Ethnic Group**

Gexu, or singing fair, is a traditional cultural activity of the Zhuang ethnic group, as well as a place for young men and women to socialize. On these occasions, young people from nearby villages will wear their finest traditional clothing and come together at Gexu to sing songs and meet their possible romantic partner. It is mainly held in the spring and autumn seasons. It is most frequently held in March and April in the spring, and usually on the third day of the third lunar month. The autumn fairs are typically held in August and September of the lunar calendar, especially during the Mid-autumn Festival. Gexu was included in the National Intangible Cultural Heritage List on May 20, 2006.

## IX. Check List

| Key Words | | | | |
|---|---|---|---|---|
| coastal | urban | rural | access | tourist center |
| metropolis | infrastructure | architecture | gateway | Life Cycle |
| coordination | rejuvenation | seasonality | community | capacity |
| cycling | hiking | trail | district | livable city |
| landmark | skyscraper | slum | moat | folk customs |
| downtown | suburb | hang out | landscape | city pass |
| **Useful Sentences** | | | | |
| 1. It is a lifetime experience!<br>2. The New York City can't be missed out.<br>3. We have a free map / information booklet for the city. Would you like one? | | | | |

4. Guilin Office of the Eighth Route Army is open to the public without admission charges.
5. The museum is open until 4:00 p. m. .
6. You can take a hop-on hop-off sightseeing bus.
7. You can appreciate the amazing night view around the city if you take the night view sightseeing bus.
8. You can hang out in pubs with live music.
9. Yangshuo is 66 kilometers to the south of Guilin.
10. Buses run from Guilin Bus Station to Yangshuo every 20 minutes from 7:00 a. m. to 8:00 p. m. .
11. Cycling along the country trails can get you a close contact with local people and allow you to gain insight into their lives.
12. City pass is a pre-paid ticket booklet with admission tickets to a handful of the most popular tourist destinations in major cities.
13. With Shanghai city pass, you can choose attractions from 18 of Shanghai's greatest attractions.
14. It is valid for 365 days after your purchase and is automatically activated after its first use.
15. You can also enjoy unlimited free travel on Shanghai City Sightseeing Tour Bus.
16. You can enjoy some discount when shopping or having dinner in designated stores or restaurants.

# Unit 7
# Tourist Attraction

**Learning Objectives**

After learning this part, you should be able to:
1. understand the role that attractions play in the development of tourism industry.
2. be able to wirte a commentary and give an introduction of an attraction.
3. understand the theory of clear waters and green moutains are invaluable assets and develop the concept of ecological development.

## | Lead In

Classify the following attractions into corresponding category.

| | | | |
|---|---|---|---|
| The Great Wall | Yangtze River | Terra—cotta Warriors | Mount Huangshan |
| Olympic Games | Temple of Heaven | The Grand Canal | Potala Palace |
| Jiuzhaigou Valley | Mogao Grottoes | Three Paralled Rivers of Yunnan | |
| Water-Splashing Festival | Longsheng Rice Terraces | Beijing Planetarium | |
| Silver beach | Oriental Pearl Tower | Disneyland | Beijing Opera show |

| Natural Attraction | Cultural Attraction |
|---|---|
|  |  |

## 📖 Background Reading

### Tourist Attraction

Attractions provide the single most important reason for leisure tourism to a destination. Attractions are the reason people travel. Without attractions drawing tourists to destinations, there would be little need for all other tourism services such as transportation, lodging, food, distribution, and so on.

A **tourist attraction** is a place of interest where tourists visit, typically for its inherent or an exhibited natural or cultural value, historical significance, natural or built beauty, offering leisure and amusement.

Natural attractions are the "mainsprings" that drive many people to travel. Natural resources included beaches, tropical islands, mountains, deserts and forests, rivers and lakes, wildlife, and outstanding natural phenomena as aurora, sunrise and sunset, cloud sea and so on. The great national parks of the United States and other countries, such as those in China, Canada, India, Australia, and Japan, are examples. These natural wonders lure travelers to enjoy the natural beauty, recreation, and inspiration that they provide.

Cultural tourist attractions include historical places, monuments, ancient temples, zoos, aquaria museums, and art galleries, botanical gardens, buildings and structures (such as forts, castles, libraries, former prisons, skyscrapers, bridges), theme parks and carnivals, living history museums, public art (sculptures, statues, murals), ethnic enclave communities, historic trains and cultural events. They have appeal to those inspired to learn more about contemporary and long-vanished civilization.

Recreation attractions maintain and provide access to indoor and outdoor facilities where people can participate in sports and other recreational activities. Examples include swimming pools, bowling alleys, ice skating rinks, golf courses, ski resorts, hiking trails, bicycle paths, and marinas. Sports events such as a soccer game, Formula 1 race or sailing regatta can also attract tourists.

Commercial attractions are retail operations dealing in gifts, handcrafted goods, art, and souvenirs that attract tourists. Recent surveys show that shopping is the number-one activity participated in by both domestic and international visitors.

Factory tours, industrial heritage, creative art and crafts workshops are the object of cultural niches like industrial tourism and creative tourism. Wineries and breweries have long been tourist attractions. Factory tours are growing in number, and manufacturers have developed elaborate facilities to handle tourists. An example is the Waterford Crystal Factory in Ireland, which houses a world-class crystal museum. The vast oil sands mining operations in Northern Alberta, Canada, now attracts many visitors for both professional and personal reasons.

Great modern cities with their cultural treasures of many sorts provide powerful attractions to millions of visitors each year. Many tourist attractions are landmarks of cities. Times Square in New York, Fisherman's Wharf in San Francisco, and Navy Pier in Chicago combine the appeal of a large city with shopping, dining, culture, and entertainment to attract millions of visitors each year. Sightseeing tours are provided in most cities, giving easy access to the city's attractions.

While some tourist attractions provide visitors a memorable experience for a reasonable admission charge or even for free, others may be of low quality and overprice their goods and services (such as admission, food, and souvenirs) in order to profit excessively from tourists. Such places are commonly known as tourist traps.

Attractions also serve a variety of different purposes, since for many their origins had nothing to do with tourism. For example, attractions often have an explicit educational purpose, are frequently central to the protection, or in fact creation, of cultural identities, and can contribute to the conservation and protection of many historic sites.

## Tourism Carrying Capacity

According to WTO, **tourism carrying capacity** is the maximum number of people that may visit a tourist destination at the same time, without causing destruction of the physical, economic, social-cultural environment and an unacceptable decrease in the quality of visitors' satisfaction.

The tourism industry, especially in national parks and protected areas, is subject to the concept of carrying capacity so as to determine the scale of tourist activities which can be sustained at specific times in different places.

The concepts of carrying capacity are now generally accepted, but difficulties in measuring and quantifying the thresholds have restricted the use of carrying capacity as a planning tool. Some factors causing this restriction are: the acceptable levels of crowding can differ from one society to another; certain types of developments necessitate higher densities than others, even if the sizes of the developments are the same, e.g. beaches for relaxation vis-a-vis tourism; and physical and environmental carrying capacities can be affected by management techniques.

## Situational Dialogues

### ➢ Dialogue 1

**At the Ticket Office**

Scene: At the ticket office of a park, the staff (A) is answering the guest's (B) question.

A: Good morning, madam. May I help you?

B: I bought two admission tickets of your park from Ctrip. Do I need to exchange paper tickets here?

A: You can get access to the park directly by scanning the QR code you get from your purchase.

B: By the way, are there any interpretation services in the park?

A: We offer two kinds of interpretation service. You can hire a tour guide who will show you around the park and interact with you or you can rent a self-service audio guide device here for 20 yuan each. You will hear interpretation when approaching the scenic spot.

B: How much is the tour guide service?

A: It is RMB 100 yuan per time.

B: OK, I will take one. Here is the money.

A: Here is your receipt. The tour guide will meet you at the entrance.

B: Thank you.

A: You're welcome. Have a nice day!

### ➢ Dialogue 2

**At the Elephant Trunk Hill Park**

Scene: A tour group headed by a tour guide (A) enters the Elephant Trunk Hill Park. The guide is giving an introduction to the tourists (B) about the park.

A: Ladies and gentlemen, here we are at the Elephant Trunk Hill Park. Before getting off the coach, I would like to say something about our tour. Firstly, we will stay here for about one and a half hours, I hope everybody could meet again at the entrance of the park at 11:30 a.m.; secondly, please remember my cell number in case of any problems. My number is 13907735678; finally, please take care of your money and yourself anytime and anywhere. Now do you have any questions?

B: No.

A: All right. Now, please get off the bus and don't forget to bring your valuables with you.

(After entering the entrance)

A: Before we begin our tour, please take a look at the sketch map of the park. This is where we are(point to the mark). Elephant Trunk Hill is the landmark of Guilin. It is located on the western bank of Li River. Do you know why this park is so named? I'll leave this question for you to explore. Now follow me, please.

B: What a beautiful garden!

A: Well, ladies and gentlemen, use your imagination please. Do you find the elephant? Yes, it is just over there. The hill got the name because of its unique shape, it looks like a huge elephant sucking up water from Li River with its long trunk.

B: Oh, it is amazing! Look! There is a cave there!

A: Well, that cave is called Water Moon Cave , and it is between the trunk and the legs, which is a semi-round cave penetrated by water. When the water is still and calm, the cave and its reflection form a full moon. This phenomenon is unique and many laudatory inscriptions were found on the wall inside the cave.

B: What a lovely view! Let's climb up the hill to get a better view of the surroundings.

A: All right. Let's go.

> **Dialogue 3**

**At the Museum**

Scene: Steven (A) and May (B) pay a visit to the museum of historical relics.

A: May, is this the Hall of Ancient China?

B: Yes. Look at these historical relics here, amazing!

A: Why are they all in glass boxes?

B: For protection. Some relics will turn to dust if they were exposed to air.

A: So there is no air in the glass boxes?

B: No, there isn't. There is a vacuum in every box.

A: I wonder how old these things are. Thousands of years?

B: They all come from a very ancient time. Use your cell phone and scan the QR code on the label, you can find out their histories and stories.

A: Wow! This porcelain vase was made as a gift for Emperor Qianlong's birthday. Let me take a picture of it.

B: Don't use your flash!

A: Hey, look at the tripod. I've seen it on TV.

B: It was made 4000 years ago. It's priceless!

## Ⅳ Chinese Stories

### The Forbidden City

The Forbidden City, situated in the very heart of Beijing, was home to 24 emperors of the Ming and Qing Dynasties. The Forbidden City is the best preserved imperial palace in China and the largest ancient palatial structure in the world. In 1987 it was listed as a UNESCO World Heritage Site.

The Forbidden City was constructed between 1406 and 1420 by the Ming emperor Zhu Di and witnessed the enthronement of 14 Ming and 10 Qing emperors over the following 505 years. The Forbidden City is surrounded by 10-metre-high walls and a 52-metre-wide moat. Measuring 961 meters from north to south and 753 meters from east to west, the complex covers an area of 1120000 square meters. It consists of 70 palaces and courtyards, 980 buildings and 8704 rooms. To represent the supreme power of the emperor given from God, and the place where he lived being the center of the world, all the gates, palaces and other structures of the Forbidden City were arranged about the south-north central axis of Beijing.

The Meridian Gate is the main entrance to the Forbidden City. It is called Meridian Gate because the emperor believed that the meridian line went right through the Forbidden City and his imperial residence was the center of the whole universe. Meridian Gate was the place where the Emperor announced the new lunar calendar on the winter solstice. The gate has 5 openings. The central passage is for the emperor only. But the empress could use it once on the wedding ceremony. The top three scholars of the palace examination were allowed to go through it on the day of result announcement.

Entering the Meridian Gate, there are five marble bridges, Golden Stream Bridge, on the Inner Golden Water River. The five bridges were supposed to represent the five virtues preached by Confucius—benevolence, righteousness, manners, wisdom and credit.

Since yellow is the symbol of the royal family, it is the dominant color in the Forbidden City. Roofs are built with yellow glazed tiles; decorations in the palace are painted yellow; even the bricks on the ground are made yellow by a special process. However, there is one exception. Wenyuange, the royal library, has a black roof. The reason is that it was believed that black represented water then and could extinguish fire.

The Forbidden City falls into two parts: the Outer Court and the Inner Court. The Outer Court was the venue for the emperor's court and grand audiences.

There is a big square courtyard in front of the Hall of Supreme Harmony, covering an area of 30000 square meters. In the old days, when the grand ceremonies were held in the Hall of Supreme Harmony, the ceremonial guards would stand in the courtyard in lines. During the ceremony the emperor sat on the throne, while the civil and military officials would stand in the courtyard, kneeling down in front of the emperor.

The Outer Court is made up of three main buildings, the Hall of Supreme Harmony, the Hall of Central Harmony and the Hall of Preserving Harmony. These halls were where the emperors attended the grand ceremonies and conducted state affairs.

The first hall is the Hall of Supreme Harmony, the most important and largest structure in the Forbidden City. The name of Supreme Harmony comes for the Book of Changes. It means the relations of various things in the universe would be in perfect harmony, especially the relations between the emperors and officials. Here the emperor held grand ceremonies such as the emperor's enthronement ceremony, the wedding ceremony, dispatched generals to the battles, and the emperor received the successful candidates of the imperial examination, etc. Also, the emperor held grand feasts each year on New Year's Day, winter solstice and his own birthday.

Behind the Hall of Supreme Harmony is the Hall of Central Harmony, the resting place of the emperor before presiding over grand events held in the Hall of Supreme Harmony. Emperors would rehearse their speeches and presentations here before departing to the Temple of Heaven for the sacrifice rites.

The last hall is the Hall of Preserving Harmony which was used for banquets on each New Year's Eve and the 15th day of the lunar month to entertain the civil and military officials, the princes and envoys of the Mongolian nobles and other nationalities. The Imperial Palace Exam was held here once every three years in the Qing Dynasty.

Behind the Hall of Preserving Harmony, there is a big Marble Ramp, carved with mountain cliffs, sea waves, clouds and nine dragons. It is 16.57 meters long, 3.07 meters wide and 1.7 meters thick, and weighs about 250 tons.

The Gate of Heavenly Purity, where emperors from Kangxi to Xianfeng in Qing Dynasty sat on the throne hearing reports and making decisions, is the main gate of the Inner Court.

The Inner Court is composed of the three main structures at the rear of the Forbidden City, namely the Palace of Heavenly Peace, the Hall of Union and the Palace of Earthly Tranquility. Besides the three main buildings there are the Six Eastern Palaces and Six Western Palaces, where the emperor used to handle everyday affairs, and which was the living quarters of the emperor and his family. The Inner Court is not only comprised of the residences of the emperor and his consorts, but also venues for religious rituals and administrative activities.

The Palace of Heavenly Peace was where the 14 emperors of the Ming Dynasty and the first two emperors of the Qing Dynasty lived and handle the daily affairs. Here was also the place for holding the mourning service for the deceased emperor. The famous "banquet of thousand aged people" was held twice here in the Qing Dynasty.

The Hall of Union was the place where the empress held the important ceremonies and her birthday celebration. The empress usually received greetings from the concubines, princes and princesses on her birthday celebration. This is also the place where the imperial seals were stored.

The Palace of Earthly Tranquility was used as the residence for the empresses during the Ming and early Qing Dynasties. During the Qing Dynasty, the western chamber became the wedding chamber for the emperor.

The far north end of the Inner Court is the Imperial Garden. The garden offers an aesthetic change from the crimson and gray building complex to a colorful and luxuriant atmosphere.

The Gate of Divine Prowess is the north gate of the Forbidden City.

## Ⅴ Listening

**1. Listen to the conversation and fill in the blanks.**

**Expo Park**

A: Charlie   B: Roy

A: How is your visit to the Expo Park?

B: It's splendid. Over 200 countries participated in this Expo. _____ _____.

A: That's not surprising at all. News report says the Expo Park _____ _____. Which pavilions did you visit?

B: We went to China Pavilion. _____ _____. It's amazing. My favorite pavilion is the Future of the City Pavilion. It _____.

A: "_____" is the theme of Shanghai Expo.

B: Indeed. I also like the National Grid Pavilion very much. It _____ _____ for visitors. I won't tell you the details, _____ _____.

A: _____. Now I've made up my mind to go.

B: Good. _____.

Unit 7    Tourist Attraction

2. **Listen to the dialogue and judge true (T) or false (F) for each statement.**

### National Park in the United States

(1) The first national park in the world is Yellow Stone which was established in 1972. (    )

(2) Over 100000 national parks and protected areas have been established in more than 100 countries for the enjoyment of people today and generations to come. (    )

(3) The national park services in the United States manage over 400 units that cover an area of 34 million hectares of land. (    )

(4) Two main jobs of the National Park Service is to protect the national parks and to help visitors enjoy them.

(5) All the national parks charge entrance fee. (    )

(6) The entrance fee is good for a week. (    )

(7) People over 60-years-old can buy a lifetime pass for $10. (    )

## Ⅵ Speaking

1. **Discussion: Discuss the features of different tourist attractions with your partner. Take notes and share in the class.**

| The features of different attractions | |
|---|---|
| Disneyland | |
| The Great Wall | |
| Li River | |
| Lijiang Ancient Town | |

2. **Role play: Work in pairs and act out the following dialogues.**

(1) Mike is a tour guide. He is delivering a on-the-way introduction to an American tour group when they are heading for Yangshuo.

(2) John works in Shanghai Disneyland. He is answering a guest's question about show time and directions.

(3) Lily works in a art gallery. She is answering guest's inquiry about the exhibition.

# VII Writing

## Tour Commentary

### 1. Writing Skills

Delivering a speech in a scenic spot or park is an important part of guiding service. Identifying relevant information for the tour commentary is important. The content of the tour commentary should provide interesting tidbits and facts to promote your country. It should be informative and educational. Most importantly, good stories are part of great tour commentary. Good stories will keep the travelers entertained, engaged and most important of all, provide an enjoyable experience to tourists.

A good commentary should introduce more knowledge except for the basic facts, such as famous poets, compliments by celebrities, or similar attractions. Vivid and expressive language should be used in the commentary, colloquial phrase are easy to understand than the written expressions.

### 2. Sample

#### The Museum of Terra-cotta Warriors

Good morning, ladies and gentlemen, so nice to see you. I'm your interpreter in the museum of Terra-cotta Warriors. This museum is located at the foot of Mountain Li Shan, about 35 kilometers east of Xi'an. First I will give you a brief introduction about the master of this underground army—The First Qin Emperor. His name was Ying Zheng. He came to the throne at the age of 13 in 246 B.C. and seized the power at the age of 22 in 237 B.C. By 221 B.C. when he was only 38 years old, he had annexed all the six independent states and established the first feudal empire in the long history of China.

As soon as he came to the throne, he ordered that a magnificent mausoleum should be built for him. And after the unification of the whole country, he even gathered 720000 conscripts from all parts of the country to work on his mausoleum. In fact, it took 37 years to complete this project. And the site of these Terra-cotta Warriors and horses is just a small part of his mausoleum.

Pit 1 was discovered in March 1974 when some local farmers were digging a water well to save them from the drought. There are about 6000 figures in this large pit if fully excavated according to the density. But today, only one third has been excavated.

Pit 1, the largest pit, is in rectangular shape. It measures 230 meters long from east to west, 62 meters wide from north to south and 5 meters deep, covering an area of 14260 m². It is an earth and wood structure in the shape of a tunnel. Five sloping roadways were constructed on 4 sides of pit to permit access. But do you know how did Qin people make such a large underground construction? Let me tell you the story. First, a large pit was made. The floor was paved with bricks. Earth walls were built and pillars were erected. There are 10 partition walls dividing the whole pit into 11 corridors. On top of the pillars were crossbeams and the crossbeams were covered with mats and then earth. After finishing the underground building, the 6000 pottery figures were sent to the corridors through the slopping roadways. Then the entrances were sealed. Unfortunately, someone set a big fire on the underground building, the thousands figures were destroyed into fragments at the end of the Qin Dynasty.

The layout of this pit is a large military battle formation. After months to years of careful and painstaking restoration, the figures are displayed at their original shape and location. The Terra-cotta Warriors and horses were big in life-size and exquisitely made with high technology. The height of the Terra-cotta Warriors varies from 1.78 m, the shortest, to 1.97 m, the tallest. They look healthy and strong and have different facial expressions. Probably they were sculpted by craftsmen according to real soldiers of the Qin Dynasty. Look carefully, it seems that we can still feel the slight breath when approaching them!

Once the Terra-cotta Warriors and horses were all arranged inside the corridors, the entrances were closed. It meant a sealed united army was formed to guard Emperor Qinshihuang's underground palace.

Thousands of real weapons were unearthed from these terra-cotta army pits, including broad knives, swords, spears, dagger-axes, halberds, bows, crossbows and arrowheads. These weapons were exquisitely made. Some of them are still very sharp, analyses show that they are made of alloys of copper and tin, containing more than ten kinds of other metals. Since their surfaces were treated with chromium, they are as bright as new, though buried underground for more than 2000 years. This indicates that Qin Dynasty's metallurgical technology and weapon-manufacturing technique already reached quite a high level.

In December, 1980, 2 sets of large painted bronze chariots and horses were unearthed 20 meters west of the mausoleum. Having remained for more than 2200 years, the 2 bronze chariots and horses were broke into more than 3000 pieces. After 8 years of careful and painstaking restoration, they have been restored to their original shape and now are displayed in our museum. The bronze chariots and horses are half the size of the real ones. These 2 sets of bronze chariots and horses provide a lot of precious information to help the study of the harnessing and driving system of the single-shaft-two-wheeled chariot of Qin Dynasty, and help solve many of the longtime questions in dispute. One such question concerns the reins. It was said "A charioteer holds 6 reins", but in the Qin Dynasty, a four-horse-drawn chariot has eight reins, two for each horse. So the question that has puzzled historians for centuries is that which 6 reins were held by the charioteer. Now the unearthing of the Qin bronze chariots and horses has brought to light the answer. From these chariots, we can see that the 6 reins held by the charioteers are the 4 reins of the side horses, while the inside reins of the middle horses are tied to the front part of the chariot, these bronze chariots and horses present us a clear picture of the ancient harnessing and driving system.

These 2 sets of bronze chariots are the earliest, largest and most complete structure of their kind ever discovered in China. They are just a small part of all the treasures buried in the mausoleum of Emperor Qinshihuang. We can predict that there will be more and more exciting archaeological finds around the tomb area.

Well, there are so many wonderful things for you to explore, you can walk around and take some pictures. Please pay attention to safety!

**3. Writing Practice**

Choose a tourist attraction and write a tour commentary.

# Ⅷ Supplementary Reading

**Theme Park**

Theme park is a term for a group of rides and other entertainment attractions assembled for the purpose of entertaining a large group of people. A theme park is differentiated from an amusement park by its various "lands" (sections) devoted to telling a particular story. These lands are characterized by the idea that the immersive environment they create with architecture, landscaping, stores, rides, and even food that support a specific theme. Visual intrusions from other "lands", or from outside the park, are considered undesirable. Non-theme amusement park rides will usually have little in terms of theming or additional design elements. Also, a single themed attraction by itself does not qualify an amusement park as a theme park. It takes a multiplicity of elements in a common area to define "lands", and numerous lands to constitute a theme park. The original theme park and archetype of the designation is Disneyland in Anaheim, California.

**National Park**

A national park is a tract of land declared public property by a national government with a view to its preservation and development for purposes of recreation and culture, or an area of countryside for public use designated by a national government as being of notable scenic, environmental, or historical importance. Often it is a reserve of natural, semi-natural, or developed land that a sovereign state declares or owns. Although individual nations designate their own national parks differently, there is a common idea: the conservation of wild nature for posterity and as a symbol of national pride. The United States established the first "public park or pleasuring-ground for the benefit and enjoyment of the people", Yellowstone National Park, in 1872.

National parks are almost always open to visitors. Most national parks provide outdoor recreation and camping opportunities as well as classes designed to educate the public on the importance of conservation and the natural wonders of the land in which the national park is located.

## The Great Wall

There is an old saying in China that "He who has never been to the Great Wall is not a true man". The Great Wall was the military project built to ward off invasion of the north horde in ancient China. With the length of 8851.8 km, the width of 4-5 meters and the height of 6-7 meters, the Great Wall crosses 8 provinces including Hebei, Beijing, Inner Mongolia, Shanxi, Shaanxi, Ningxia, Gansu and Liaoning. The construction history of the Great Wall could be traced back to 9 B.C.. In 220 B.C., under the reign of Emperor Qinshihuang, sections of earlier fortifications were joined together to form a united defence system against invasions from the north. Construction continued up to the Ming Dynasty (1368-1644), when the Great Wall became the world's largest military structure.

This wall often traces the crest lines of hills and mountains as it snakes across the Chinese countryside, and about one-fourth of its length consists solely of natural barriers such as rivers and mountain ridges. The Great Wall is not an individual rampart but an integrated defense system formed by fortifications including ramparts, watch towers, beacon towers, barrier walls, battle walls, fortresses and passes, etc.

The Great Wall was designated a UNESCO World Heritage Site in 1987.

## Mogao Grottoes

Mogao Grottoes (also known as "Thousand Buddha Grottoes") was first constructed in 366 A.D. and were continuously built for around 1000 years across 11 dynasties or periods. It represents the great achievement of Buddhist art from the 4th to the 14th century. In 1987, Mogao Grottoes were enlisted by the UNESCO in the first batch of World Heritage List of China.

Mogao Grottoes are located on the eastern slope of Mingsha Mountain and the west bank of Dangquan River, which is 25 kilometers to the southeast of Dunhuang City. Distributed on a cliff of about two kilometers long south to north and about 15 to 30 meters high, Mogao Grottoes were built on rocks of Jiuquan gravel stratum.

Spanning a distance of over 1600 meters, the grottoes are composed of 735 caves (including 492 containing murals and painted statues), housing about 45000 square meters of murals and more than 2000 painted sculptures. Mogao Grottoes represent the integration of the diversified cultures and civilizations along the Silk Road.

**The Recreational Vehicle (RV)**

The recreational vehicle is a nickname for a whole family of recreational vehicles that combine transportation and temporary living quarters for recreation, camping and travel. Americans are the largest market segment for the RV industry to-date, with over 40 million people reporting that they take part in some form of recreational vehicle camping activities at least once during the year. The great thing about RV travel is that you're at home and away at the same time! RV travel allows you to pursue adventures into unknown places and also paradoxically allows you to do so in the comfort of a familiar environment.

**Siheyuan**

Siheyuan is Beijing's traditional form of residence. The layout of small four-section compound is simple. Generally speaking, Siheyuan often has three rooms in the north, most of them are cut off into two or three parts which are divided into light and dark. The main rooms are full of sunshine in the winter. They are cool in summers and warm in winters. There are two wing-rooms in each side of the east and west. Three rooms (also known as block back room) are in the south and the eastern side of south is open for the door. The door is often made as a gate tower and there are paths which are made of bricks lead to each room.

## IX Check List

| Key Words | | | | |
|---|---|---|---|---|
| attraction | scenery | heritage | day trip | carrying capacity |
| mosque | church | palace | pavilion | nature reserve |
| statue | grotto | canal | gallery | summer resort |
| exposition | planetarium | museum | aquarium | amusement park |
| temple fair | pagoda | monastery | temple | classical garden |
| castle | mural | fort | sculpture | theme park |

| stadium | concert hall | fountain | skyscraper | former residence |
|---|---|---|---|---|
| volcano | iceberg | glacier | canyon | hot spring |
| stalactite | swamp | cliff | beach | national forest |
| waterfall | tide | valley | stream | folk customs |
| habitat | hill | rock | grassland | sketch map |
| guardrail | cable car | campsite | admission | ticket office |

**Useful Sentences**

**On the way to the scenic spot**

1. Are all the people here?
2. Can you hear me at the back?
3. Today we are going to visit the Seven Star Park.
4. Now we are heading for it.
5. It takes about 1 hour's drive to get there.
6. There are a lot of relics there.
7. We'll have our lunch on the boat while touring the lake.
8. The limousine will return to the hotel at 5:40 p.m..
9. You will have a good chance to feast your eyes in the park.

**In the park**

1. It will need one and a half hours to visit the whole scenery. Let's begin from here.
2. The ticket office is over there through the gate on your right.
3. The admission fee is 30 yuan for an adult.
4. We have tickets half price for children under 1.4 meters.
5. Would you please show your certificate for half-price ticket?
6. You can get access to the park directly by scanning the QR code you get from your purchase.
7. It is a all-in-one ticket.
8. Please insert it in this slot with the arrow up.
9. Our tourist site has access to wheelchairs.
10. Due to equipment maintenance, some facilities are not available today.
11. You can walk around freely and please remember we will collect just here on twelve o'clock.
12. Please be careful when you climb the mountain, it is rather steep.
13. If you don't like climbing by yourself, you can take the cable car.
14. I'm sure everybody can make it.
15. You can go as far as you like.
16. This is the furthest point we can go.
17. I'll leave you 10 minutes for taking pictures.
18. Now you can look around on your own for a while.

19. Here is the best spot for pictures.
20. Shall we have a group picture taken here?
21. Now, don't move. I'm focusing the lens. Everybody say cheese, please!
22. We'll meet half an hour later at the entrance and will go down-hill, by the same way as where we came up.
23. I hate to push you. Would you mind moving a little faster?
24. I'm afraid we are behind schedule.
25. One third of this area is covered with forest. Please walk on the plank path instead of trampling on grass.
26. Green mountains roll over one another.
27. Please watch your step.
28. Shall I give you a hand?

**At a museum**

1. This museum can accommodate 1000 people.
2. There is a bronze exhibition on the second floor gallery.
3. It opens at 10 o'clock in the morning every day.
4. The museum provides free interpretation service at every hour sharp.
5. The gallery is exhibiting a series of portraits.
6. Excuse me, could you please lower your voice?
7. You can take pictures, but no flashes, please.
8. Use your cell phone and scan the QR code on the label, you can find out their histories and stories.
9. Here is a brochure for the exhibition.

# Unit 8
# Recreation and Entertainment

**Learning Objectives**

After learning this part, you should be able to:
1. get a knowledge of traditional entertainment and recreation in China.
2. be able to recommend different entertainments and recreations for tourists.
3. understand the basic concept of TCM and can deliver a brief introduction.
4. develop a strong cultural confidence by learning how to introduce the excellent folk cultures.

## | Lead In

Match the best meaning given below with the expressions that follow.

| cross talk | talk show | circus | acrobatics |
| opera | documentary | soap opera | sketch comedy |

a. _____ is a serial drama on television that examines the lives of many characters, usually focusing on emotional relationships to the point of melodrama.

b. _____ is a traditional Chinese comedic monologue or dialogue.

c. _____ is an art form in which singers and musicians perform a dramatic work combining text and musical score, usually in a theatrical setting.

d. _____ is a nonfictional motion picture intended to document some aspect of reality, primarily for the purposes of instruction, education, or maintaining a historical record.

e. _____ is a TV program or radio program where one person (or group of people) discusses various topics put forth by a host.

f. _____ is a traveling company of performers that may include acrobats, clowns, trained animals, and other novelty acts.

g. _____ comprises a series of short comedy scenes, called "sketches". Such sketches are performed by a group of comic actors or comedians, either on stage or through an audio or visual medium such as radio and television.

h. _____ is the performance of extraordinary feats of balance, agility, and motor coordination.

## Background Reading

### Entertainment in China

Since China's reform and opening-up policy in 1979, the nightlife in this country has become varied and more colorful. Nowadays, for international travelers it's easy to fill their nights during their stay in China. Experience Peking Opera or spend a night dancing at a club, or even go local, and give karaoke a try. Nightlife in China is vibrant, stunning and full of fun.

Traditional Chinese opera was a combination of dancing, singing, and acting. In ancient China, it was a form of entertainment for both men and women, the young and the old, the rich and the poor. There were five branches of traditional Chinese opera, including the Beijing Opera, Yueju, Huangmei Opera, Pingju, and Yu Opera respectively.

**Peking Opera**

Peking Opera is a national treasure with a history of 200 years. It is a synthesis of stylized action, singing, dialogue and mime, acrobatic fighting and dancing to represent a story or depict different characters and their feelings of gladness, anger, sorrow, happiness, surprise, fear and sadness.

There are four types of actor's roles: the Sheng, Dan, Jing and Chou. Each is subdivided: the Sheng are the leading male actors and they play officials, warriors, etc. They are divided into the Laosheng who wear beards and represents old men and the Xiaosheng who represents young men. The Wusheng plays soldiers and other fighters and because of this they are specially trained in acrobatics. The Dan are the female roles: the Laodan are the elderly, dignified ladies—the mothers and the widows. The Qingyi are aristocratic ladies in elegant costumes. The Huadan are the ladies' maids, usually in brightly-colored costumes. The Daomadan are the warrior women and the Caidan are the female comedians. Traditionally, female roles were played by male actors. The Jing are the painted-face roles, and they represent warriors, heroes, statesmen, adventurers and demons. The counterparts are the Fu-jing—ridiculous figures who are anything but heroic. Lastly, the Chou are basically the clowns, often performing as servants or peasants.

Apart from the singing and music, the opera also uses acrobatics and mime. Few props are used so each move, gesture or facial expression is symbolic; a whip with silk tassels indicates an actor riding a horse, lifting a foot means going through a doorway. Language is often archaic Chinese, music is earsplitting, but the costumes and makeup are magnificent. The only action that really catches the western eye is a swift battle sequence—the women warriors involved are trained acrobats, who leap, twirl, twist and attack.

The Beijing Opera band mainly consists of orchestra band and percussion band. The former frequently accompanies peaceful scenes while the latter often follows scenes of war and fighting. The commonly used percussion instruments include castanets, drums, bells and cymbals. The orchestral instruments mainly compose of the Erhu, the Huqin, the Yueqin, the Sheng, the Pipa and other instruments. The band usually sits on the left side of the stage.

The types of facial make-ups in Peking Opera are rich and various, depicting different characters and remarkable images. Moreover, there are numerous fixed editions of facial make-up. The designs of these masks are given various meanings and implications. That is to say that there exists the leading color in each of the masks, which referred to the color applied to the forehead or the cheek areas of the face. The colors of black, white and red form the basis most of the time, while these colors of purple, blue, green, yellow, pink, gold and silver play the leading role at chosen sometimes.

## Acrobatics Show

As per the historical records and ancient relics, the Chinese acrobatics originated in the period of the Warring States. Artists developed a wide repertoire and called "the show of a hundred tricks" during the Qin and Han Dynasties. Later, a variety of acrostic performance such as traditional conjuring, vocal imitation, taming animals and horsemanship have been described in books and historical relics. As musical accompany, costumes, props and lighting have been improved, acrobatics have become a comprehensive stage art, performed by more than 100 troupes throughout China.

Acrobatics are a performing art which combines physical strength and skill. The Encyclopedias Britannica describes acrobatics as "the specialized and ancient art of jumping, tumbling and balancing, often using apparatus such as poles, unicycles, balls, barrels, tightropes, trampolines and flying trapezes". Most popular programs include group contortion, jar juggling, plate spinning, bench balance, pagoda of bowls, chair stack, The Tower of Chairs and more.

### China's Nightlife

Most of the magnificent nightlife venues in China are located at the downtown of the city. Numerous hangout points offer various nightlife entertainments like dramas, acrobatics, night shows, ballet dances, karaoke or a music concert. The exploration of nightlife remains incomplete without visiting the bars and pubs. Most of the bars remain open till 4:00 a.m.. From grunge to cocktail, jazz to lounge bars, China has everything. There are bars of all shapes and sizes, some hidden in old houses, some high up in tall buildings. Sanlitun and Hou Hai in Beijing are the two most popular bar streets, while in Shanghai, popular areas lie in Xintiandi, Hengshan Road and the Bund. Bars are wonderful places where the West meets the East. You can sit back and have the good time!

Moreover, you can choose to take a night cruise to enjoy the fantastic neon-lights view, simply wander around at the local night market, and appreciate amazing local shows like the Tang Dancing Show in Xi'an, Dynamic Yunnan show in Kunming, Impression Liu Sanjie show in Yangshuo.

## Situational Dialogue

### Dialogue 1

#### Laoshe Tea House

Scene: Mr. Brown (B) wants to know more about traditional Chinese culture. His tour escort Wang (A) recommends the performance at Laoshe Tea House in Beijing.

A: How do you like the Hutong tour today, Mr. Brown?

B: It is wonderful. Is there any other opportunities that I can learn more about Chinese culture?

A: Would you like to watch a show this evening at Laoshe Tea House?

B: Is there any special meaning for Laoshe?

A: The tea house is named after renowned Chinese writer Laoshe who is famous for his drama *Tea House*, a vivid portrayal of the social dimensions of old Beijing.

B: Is the tea house an old Beijing-styled environment?

A: Yes. It is a traditional Chinese style decoration. Palace lanterns hung from the ceiling and calligraphy couplets hung on the wall make you feel like you are entering an old Beijing folk museum.

B: Having tea in such an environment must be enjoyable!

A: You'll experience the authentic life of old Beijing at Laoshe Tea House: siting around a square table, sipping cups of tea and munching on local snacks, while watching a collection of Chinese traditional performances.

B: That's fantastic! Anything special about the show?

A: The show is a review of the most popular Chinese folk arts, such as cross talk, Pekin Opera, acrobatics, face changing and shadow puppets. You can also experience the Kungfu tea which the tea is served from a long-spouted pot meters away.

B: Wow, it seems fascinating. What is cross talk? Is it something like talk show in the West?

A: Not exactly! Cross talk is a traditional Chinese comedic performance in the form of a dialogue between two performers. The language, rich in puns and allusions, is delivered in a rapid, bantering style. Good cross talk performers develop an expressive speaking technique with animated body language and fine singing skills. The performance forms include joking, exaggeration of facts and demonstration of kindness and beauty through satirical medium.

B: Cool. Let's make a reservation, please.

> **Dialogue 2**

### Giving information about Impression Liu Sanjie

Scene: a travel agent (A) is answering a guest's (B) inquiry about *Impression Liu Sanjie*

A: Good afternoon. Can I help you?

B: Yes, I'm planning a vacation with my family to Yangshuo this weekend. I read about a show in your brochure which is called *Impression Liu Sanjie*. Is the show included in the package?

A: No, it isn't. You can decide whether to pay for the show or not. But I believe it is an excellent show which will bring you one of the greatest pleasure of your life.

B: What is special about the show?

A: *Impression Liu Sanjie* is an outdoor performance. What you can see are the impressions derived from the daily life of the people living around Li River. The cast of over 600 performers are local villagers and fishermen. They go farming and fishing in the daytime, and perform as actors and actress in the evening.

B: Sounds interesting.

A: You will find the world's largest natural theater with Li River as its stage and twelve mist shrouded hills as its backdrop. Mist, rain, moonlight, the hills and their inverted reflections in the river all become the ever-changing natural background.

B: Natural theatre? Where does the audience sit?

A: The viewers are seated and surrounded by green plants on terraces on natural islands in the river. The sound equipment here cannot be seen because it is in harmony with the natural environment.

B: Amazing! What is the meaning of Liu Sanjie?

A: Liu Sanjie is a fairy singer in the myths and legends of Zhuang minority. She is incomparably beautiful, and has voice to match her beauty.

B: Is the show far from Yangshuo?

A: The theatre is one mile from West Street. you can take a car for 5-10 minutes to the theater. It takes half an hour by walking.

B: How long does it last for?

A: The performance lasts for one hour.

B: How much does the show cost?

A: The price of the tickets varied from 198 to 680 yuan.

B: What time does it begin?

A: The show begins at 8:00 p.m. every night.

B: Thank you very much for your information.

A: You're welcome.

## ➢ Dialogue 3

### Traditional Chinese Medicine

Scene: Wang Lei (A) is talking about Traditional Chinese Medicine(TCM) with his American friend Mike (B)

A: Mike, guess what? The article I just read considers TCM the fifth great invention of China.

B: It works for me! More and more people have recognized its remarkable curative effect.

A: That's true. And you know what? TCM's contribution to the world is not only an original medical system but also a part of China's traditional culture.

B: Yeah! I read some introductions for TCM. Some of the basic theories are so difficult to understand, such as the concept of Yin and Yang.

A: It is difficult for a foreigner to understand Chinese traditional philosophy. But the key point is to keep balance and harmony, whether inside or outside your body.

B: That is a wonderful idea! I think TCM is superior to western medicine in regarding human body as a whole and interacting with the surroundings.

A: Right. TCM is such a broad and deep system. It deserves more attention and study.

B: I'm trying to learn more about TCM. Would you help me sometimes?

A: Sure. Let's study together.

B: Great!

A: Traditional Chinese Medicine is really miraculous! How did people discover the invisible "meridians and collaterals" in human body?

B: Wait! Are there really such channels in our body?

A: I believe so. Acupuncture is based on the theory of "meridians and collaterals" and there are countless successful cases of acupuncture treatment.

B: I guess you are right. Still this is mysterious. Acupuncture is used to regulate or correct the flow of "Qi" to restore health. What is your understanding of "Qi", Wang?

A: To be frank, I don't think I got the concept of "Qi". In my understanding, "Qi" is a kind of energy. It is the fundamental stuff of the universe.

B: It is said that "Qi" flows throughout the body in channels. Why cannot I sense the flow?

A: Me either. It's said that people practicing Qigong can feel and regulate the flow of "Qi" in our body!

B: In my opinion, we should leave this question open. It is not wise to make a hasty judgement. Plus, we are far from knowing our body completely.

A: I am with you. Listen, Mike, how about taking a walk outside for some fresh air? Maybe it will do good to the flow of "Qi" in our body!

B: Let's go!

## IV Chinese Stories

### Traditional Chinese Medicine

**Basic Theory of TCM**

The theories of **Traditional Chinese Medicine** (TCM) are quite different from those of Western medicine. Its basic theory, including Yin and Yang, the Five-Elements, Blood and "Qi", attempts to explain the nature of life cycle and disease changes. TCM considers nature and human to form a single whole, and emphasizes the philosophical concept known as "The Unity of Heaven and Human". Environmental factors such as the four seasons and changes in temperature and weather are believed to influence the human body, with the body and nature forming an integrated system.

**Yin and Yang**

The physiology of Chinese medicine holds that the human body's life is the result of the balance of Yin and Yang. They never separate; one cannot exist without the other. This is the Yin/Yang principle of interconnectedness and interdependence. Yin is the inner and negative principles, and Yang is outer and positive principles. Seen from the recovery mechanism of organs, Yang functions to protect from outer harm, and Yin is the inner base to store and provide energy for its counterpart. The key reason why there is sickness is because the two aspects lose their harmony.

## The Five Elements

According to the Five-Elements Theory, the liver and gallbladder are wood, the heart is fire, the spleen and stomach are earth, the lungs and intestines are metal, and the kidneys and bladder are water. TCM considers that they are fundamental energies alive in nature and always in motion. These dynamic interactions enable all the organ systems to work in one harmonious, greater system. If their relationships are good, a state of wellness prevails; if any of the relationships become unbalanced, health problems result.

## Blood and "Qi"

In TCM, blood and "Qi" are inseparable. "Qi" is considered to be the force that animates and informs all things. "Qi" has two aspects: one is energy, power, or force; the other is conscious intelligence or information. Blood is the "mother" of "Qi"; it carries "Qi" and also provides nutrients for its movement. In turn, "Qi" is the "commander" of the blood. This means that "Qi" is the force that makes blood flow throughout the body and provides the intelligence that guides it to the places where it needs to be. Blood and "Qi" also affect one another and have the dynamic ability to transfer various properties back and forth.

## Major TCM Treatment Modalities

Often Westerners derive their understanding of TCM from acupuncture. However, acupuncture is only one of the major treatment modalities of this comprehensive medical system.

## Herbal Medicine

Chinese herbal medicine has played an important role in people's lives. The invention and application of Chinese medicine has a history of thousand years. It is somewhat similar to Chinese culture. It aims to prevent, diagnose and treat diseases.

It mainly consists of natural medicines and produced ones, namely medicines made from herbal, animal, mineral, some chemical substance and biological substance, which have no or little side effects. Another feature of Chinese herbal medicines is that they are mostly compound. By making the medicine with an appropriate proportion of different ingredients, the medicine can treat complicated diseases while maintaining the lowest possible side effects.

## Massage

Massage, a kind of outer physiotherapy, is to apply manipulation on the channels of human body, thus preventing disease and keeping healthy. Standard manipulation and special skills are needed to do massage. The strength used should be persistent, strong, well-distributed, mild, deep and thorough. Hand is most often used for massage but foot, forearm elbow and special tools can also do.

The ways to do massage vary, such as pulling, pushing, finger pushing, rubbing, knocking, etc. The effects of massage have been affirmed by people who have experienced, that is, relieving the bones and muscles, detumescence, acesodyne, adjusting dislocation of the joints, removal of muscle spasm and so on. Besides massages for cure, there are also ones for keeping fit. For instance, kneading the acupoints around eyes can give you a good eyesight; massaging simply and exactly on the three acupoints of head can quickly relax yourself, etc.

## Acupuncture

Acupuncture is the experiential summary undergoing the long-term struggle by the Chinese people. Actually it consists of two parts: operations with needles and ones with fire, both of them are essential and correlative during curing.

Operations with needles feature the pricks of needles on acupoints to adjust the organic functions and clear the energy channels of obstruction in our body. Once the needle enters into the acupoints, deep or shallow, lifted or entwisted, inserted in different frequency, all according to the techniques of experienced doctors, the miraculous effect will appear. This kind of treatment does not do any harm to the body nor has any side effect. Doctors handling the needle freely, it is rather convenient and comfortable because it needs no special condition or facilities, except the small and thin needles. So it is easy for patients to accept.

Operations with fire can also be dated back to the Eolithic Age. The methods in common use are moxibustion with moxa cone and cupping. The principle of cupping lies in that, when the fire in the jar is burnt, heating power ejects the air out, and the negative pressure makes the jar stick to the skin, which causes the stasis of blood to stimulate and adjust the organ functions, the moxa cone can also have this effect.

## Four Methods of Diagnosis

In Chinese medicine, doctors use various methods to get full and detailed information about the patients and to guide their treatment. To treat the diseases, they use the methods of observation, auscultation and olfaction, interrogation, and pulse feeling and palpation.

## Observation

To observe, it is believed that people's outer appearance is closely linked with their internal organs. If there is something wrong with the internal organs, such changes will be reflected in their expressions and appearance. Therefore doctors can analyze the changes of the internal organs by observing the outer appearance.

## Auscultation and Olfaction

By methods of auscultation and olfaction, doctors try to diagnose the disease by listening to the sound of the patients and smelling the odor of excreta released by human body. By listening to the sound of the patients, doctors can not only detect the changes of the organs related with sound, but also changes of other internal organs. Doctors can smell the odor released by patients. It is believed that when viruses attack human body, people's internal organs and blood will be affected, thus their body fluid and excreta will release bad smell.

## Interrogation

By interrogation, doctor will talk to the patients or someone who know the disease to get the information about how the disease occurs, how it develops, its current symptoms and how it is treated. This method is useful when there are no obvious symptoms from the patients' outer appearance. Also, by interrogating, doctors can obtain other indirect information related with the disease, such as the patients' daily life, working environment, food preference and marriage status.

## Pulse Feeling and Palpation

Doctors use the method of pulse feeling and palpation by touching or pressing the patient's pulse. It is believed that changes inside the body are reflected by the changes of the pulse activity. Sometimes doctors press the skin of certain part of the body to identify the nature and the severity of the disease inside certain part of the body.

## Ⅴ Listening

**1. Listen to the conversation and fill in the blanks.**

### Opera

A: Charlie    B: Sam

A: _____, what is it?

B: _____, composed by Mozart.

Unit 8　Recreation and Entertainment

A: Oh, it's by Mozart. It's too old for me! Who invented it anyway?

B: Opera was invented by a group of wealthy people in Florence, who _____ _____.

A: It comes from Italy, right? I mean _____, but Mozart was Austrian.

B: That's because it was so popular and spread to Germany, France, England, Russia, Spain, Portugal and other countries. But yes, _____.

A: _____?

B: Yes, even foreigners like Mozart wrote in Italian, but later as it expanded, they _____.

A: How are we supposed to know what's going on?

B: The actors also _____.

A: It seems a bit confusing to me. _____?

B: Yes, a very large one with talented performers.

A: I suppose the music will tell a story, too.

B: Yes. _____.

A: It is an interesting topic, but I think I'll _____.

**2. Listen to the dialogue and judge true (T) or false (F) for each statement.**

**Chinese Herbal Medicine**

(1) Most Chinese herbal medicine tastes bitter. (　　)

(2) Almost all of the ingredients of Chinese medicine come from natural resources, which have little side effects. (　　)

(3) Susan's grandma suffered from a neckache. (　　)

(4) The TCM doctor usually has to diagnose the patient personally to make up a prescription. (　　)

(5) There are ready-prepared pills, called "patent" herbal medicine. (　　)

扫码
听听力

## Ⅵ Speaking

**1. Discussion: Discuss the different recreational activities that are popular in Chinese and Western society with your partners. Take notes and share in the class.**

| Different recreational activities in China and the West | | |
|---|---|---|
| | China | the West |
| Sports | | |
| Opera | | |

| Dancing | | |
|---|---|---|
| Others | | |

**2. Role play. Work in pairs and act out the following dialogues.**

(1) Tom works at the recreation department of hotel. A guest would like to swim. Give him some introduction and tell him where to buy the swimming suits.

(2) Tina works in a beauty salon. Mrs. Jackson would like to have a spa treatment and facial treatment. Tina is giving her some introduction.

(3) Mr. Jackson is very interested in Chinese traditional health care. Give him an introduction on acupuncture and cupping.

## Ⅶ Practical Writing

### Invitation letter

**1. Writing Skills**

A letter of invitation is written to people inviting them for a special occasion or event in your personal and professional life. The letter has to clearly mention the event. This will help the people understand the purpose of the letter. The letter should be short and precise. A soft and polite tone should be used in the letter. The letter will begin with a welcome note and end with the details of a person whom to contact to confirm your attendance for the event.

Here are some tips for writing an invitation letter:

(1) Highlight the purpose of the gathering (meeting, conference, party, etc.).

(2) Make the reader feel his/her attendance is truly expected.

(3) Provide all the details that the recipient needs in order to attend: date, time, location, etc.

(4) Ask for a response, by a specific date if necessary.

**2. Sample**

Dear Eric,

I should be very grateful if you could join in my birthday party held in my home next Friday night. The dinner starts at 7:00 p.m., so we can have a nice and long evening.

Please let me know your decision as soon as possible.

Sincerely,
Jenny

**3. Writing Practice**

You want to invite your foreign teacher to attend the New Year party held in your classroom next weekend. Write an invitation letter.

## VIII Supplementary Reading

### Confucianism

Confucianism is a philosophy and a doctrine of ethical and social conduct based on the teachings of the great Chinese philosopher Confucius(孔子). Confucianism is based on the idea of "love" and "compassion" as two prime virtues in life. The main theme of Confucianism lays stress on the importance of individuals' moral development so that the nation can be governed by virtues rather than the use of coercive laws. Confucianism has greatly influenced the Chinese government, education, and attitudes toward correct personal behavior as well as the individual's duties to society. Confucius emphasized the importance of rituals or a code of good conduct for a society. He also emphasized that whatever the circumstances were, we always have a choice to choose the right or wrong path. If each component or individual of a society performs his part efficiently by choosing the right path, the society will be in harmony. Confucius stressed five constant virtues, namely benevolence, righteousness, manners, wisdom and credit as basic ethical code.

### Taoism

Taoism refers to a variety of related philosophical and religious traditions that have influenced East Asia for more than 1700 years. Lao Tzu is believed to be the founder of Taoism according to a number of historians. Tao—the word in simple terms means a path or a way. This thought process mainly concentrates on nature, men-cosmos correspondence, health, longevity, "Wu Wei"(action through inaction), liberty, immortality and spontaneity. Taoist ethics underline compassion, moderation and humility, which are considered to be its three jewels.

### The Theory of Five Elements

The Theory of Five Elements "wood, fire, earth, metal, and water" was an ancient philosophical concept used to explain the composition and phenomenon of the physical universe. The five elements emerged from an observation of the various groups of dynamic processes, functions and characteristics observed in the natural world. The aspects involved in each of the five elements are follows: Fire—drought, heat, flaring, ascendance, movement, etc. Wood—germination, extension, softness, harmony, flexibility, etc. Metal—strength, firmness, killing, cutting, cleaning up, etc. Earth—growing, changing, nourishing, producing, etc. Water—moisture, cold, descending, flowing, etc.

## Chinese Chess and Go

Chinese chess and Go were both strategy board games for two players.

Played on a board that was nine lines wide and ten lines long, Chinese chess had two colors: red and black. Each side had a general, advisors, elephants, horses, chariots, cannons, and soldiers. The object was to capture the enemy's general.

Go is complex. The standard board has a $19 \times 19$ grid with 361 crosses. Two players take turns to place either white or black stones. The aim is to surround a larger total area of the board than the opponent.

## Tai Chi

Tai Chi is a Chinese exercise system that uses slow, smooth body movements to achieve a state of relaxation of both body and mind. Developed originally in China as a self-defense strategy, or martial art, Tai Chi—the "supreme ultimate fist"—is practiced in modern times primarily as a gentle exercise technique. Described as "meditation in motion", Tai Chi consists of a standing person performing a series of postures or bodily movements in a slow and graceful manner, with each movement flowing without pause to the next. Properly done postures are done in a relaxed, artful, and linked way, with the circular and rhythmic movements of one position flowing seamlessly into the next.

While strict attention to body position is critical, proper breathing is considered to be equally important. Just as movements are slow and continuous and without strain, breathing should be effortless yet deep. Finally, both mental and physical balance is considered essential to Tai Chi. Altogether, the five essential qualities of Tai Chi are:

a. Slowness. To develop awareness.

b. Lightness. To make movements flow.

c. Balance. To prevent body strain.

d. Calmness. To maintain continuity.

e. Clarity. To focus the mind.

## The Eight Brocades

The Eight Brocades are a set of Qigong exercise that originated in China and are practiced throughout the world. Effectiveness of keeping fit, easy in learning and economy of exercising time are the main features of this exercise.

The characteristic of this exercise is self-stretching, with breathing coordinated to the body movement. Regular practice of this exercise can strengthen one's internal organs as well as one's muscles and tendons.

The Eight Brocades is an ideal lifetime exercise for most people. It is especially recommended for people who work at desks everyday.

**The Chinese Zodiac**

The Chinese zodiac, or Shengxiao , is a repeating cycle of 12 years, with each year being represented by an animal and its reputed attributes. In order, the 12 Chinese horoscope animals are: rat, ox, tiger, rabbit, dragon, snake, horse, goat, monkey, rooster, dog, pig.

Chinese zodiac animals have astrological and cultural meanings. Chinese people associate each animal sign with certain characteristics. It's believed that people born in a given year have the personality of that year's animal. An important use of the Chinese zodiac is to determine if two people are compatible, in a romantic relationship or any kind of relationship.

## IX Check List

| Key Words | | | | |
| --- | --- | --- | --- | --- |
| acrobatics | circus | opera | jazz | talk show |
| cinema | stage play | rap | hip hop | cross talk |
| tragedy | comedy | rock and roll | band | puppet show |
| gymnasium | health club | bowling | billiard | box office |
| sauna | massage | tennis court | aerobics | golf course |
| jogging | yoga | boxing | surfing | shadowboxing |
| hiking | cycling | ballet | chess | soap opera |
| poker | gala party | Go | mahjong | cross word |
| **Useful Sentences** | | | | |

**Entertainment Service**
1. What would you like to do this evening?
2. I can arrange it for you if you like.
3. It is free seating for the show.
4. It is "first come, first served".
5. You are allowed to take pictures during the show.
6. Here is the program.

7. Is it anything like a Western opera?
8. How do you like the show?

**At the health club**

1. Welcome to our health center/club.
2. The Fitness Center has facilities like a swimming pool, a gym, a billiard room and a bowling room. There are beauty salons, saunas and massage services, too.
3. We offer yoga, martial arts and Tai Chi classes.
4. Our service/business hours are from 3:00 p.m. to 11:00 p.m..
5. Registered guests can use the sports apparatus free of charge.
6. We have resident coach and we have another female coach for women guests, if you need help or any instruction, just call him.
7. The dressing room is in the right corner, you can have a locker there to put your clothes in.

**At the bowling room**

1. No person in slippers or drunkards is permitted to come into the bowling room and we have special bowling shoes at the service counter. We provide bowling shoes for free, your shoe size, please?
2. When the game is over, please return the shoes and you can sign your bill here.
3. What's more, children under 16 are not allowed to play the game.
4. Sorry, there is no vacant bowling lane now.

**At the swimming pool**

1. We have an indoor and an outdoor swimming pool.
2. The temperature of the water is about 26 centigrade, and we have a central heat system to keep the temperature stable.
3. The depth of the swimming pool is from 1.5 meters to 2 meters. And you can choose the deep or shallow area to swim.
4. We change the water every day and it has just been changed.
5. You can buy swimming-trunks here.

**Sauna and massage**

1. Sauna is a kind of bath that can relax in. We provide dry and wet sauna. People usually take the wet sauna.
2. We have an excellent sauna, with a free supply of towels and soap.
3. First change your shoes to slippers. Then walk up to the changing room to get prepared for a shower.
4. Please change your clothes here and take a shower before going into it. Then take a towel with you to sit inside. When it's over, go out and take a quick shower again.
5. Don't stay in the sauna room too long.
6. Those who have heart disease or high blood pressure are not allowed to take sauna, for their sake.
7. Chinese massage has a long history and it can prevent and treat various diseases by stimulating the blood circulation. I am sure you will feel better after a massage.
8. We offer massage with fragrant oils, mud baths, and all sorts of other things.
9. Maybe you have got a stiff-necked, and I'll give you a neck massage.

Unit 8  Recreation and Entertainment

10. Can you turn your head to the left/right?

**At the beauty salon**

1. Which hairstyle do you prefer?
2. How would you like your haircut, sir?
3. There are half-hour and one-hour treatments. The half-hour facial costs 150 yuan and the one hour costs 250 yuan.

# Unit 9
# Tourist Shopping

**Learning Objectives**

After learning this part, you should be able to:

1. get some knowledge of tradition Chinese handicrafts and products.

2. be able to introduce and recommend souvenirs for your guests.

3. develop a deep love for our motherland and people by studying the excellent tradtional culture and the wisdom of the working people.

## Lead In

Find the best meaning for the expressions given below.

| embroidery | brandy | batik | champagne |
| --- | --- | --- | --- |
| vodka | porcelain | pottery | cheongsam |

a. _____ is a spirit produced by distilled wine.

b. _____ is a process for printing designs on cloth. Wax is put on those areas of the cloth that you do not want to be coloured by dye.

c. _____ is a hard, shiny substance made by heating clay. It is used to make delicate cups, plates, and ornaments.

d. _____ is patterns that are sewn onto cloth using threads of various colours; cloth that is decorated in this way.

e. _____ is a straight, tightly fitting silk dress with a high neck and short sleeves and an opening at the bottom on each side, worn by women from China and Indonesia.

f. _____ is a craft involving shaping wet clays and firing them under heat to trigger a chemical transformation, hardening the clay.

g. _____ is a sparkling wine produced from grapes grown in the Champagne region of France following rules that demand, among other things, secondary fermentation of the wine in the bottle to create carbonation.

h. _____ is a clear liquor often distilled from grain or potatoes.

## ‖ Background Reading

### Tourist Shopping

Some travel the globe in search of historic locales, to eat and drink the local cuisine, or to kick back on a beautiful beach. Others are motivated by shopping for stylish goods. Whether you're looking for the most exclusive designer duds, bargain opportunities, vintage retailers or market stalls, these are many shopping paradisesin the world to visit for a shopping spree.

Shopping is a major driver of tourism worldwide, with each traveler spending an average of 813 euros ($954) on tax-free goods per trip, according to Global Blue, the tax-free refund group. Cities such as Las Vegas, Dubai, Paris, London and Singapore have "all become destinations associated with shopping tourism". Destination marketers use shopping as a tool with which to build a destination's brand equity and enhance its competitiveness. Shopping tourism benefits not only the national economy of such destinations, but also local communities, because while an upscale downtown shopping mall sells luxury international branded goods, rural farms and traditional craftspeople sell their homemade products directly to foreign tourists.

Shopping, according to the researchers, provides huge economic benefits. For instance, in Hong Kong, one of the most renowned shopping destinations worldwide, more than 60% of the HK$359 billion income from tourism is spent on shopping. Chinese mainland tourists spend a particularly large proportion of their budget on shopping—over 70%, compared with only 20% for North American tourists. Shopping also offers these tourists "enjoyable experiential value during travel" and encourages return visits.

Outbound tourism from China is to swamp the world by 2019 with a wave of 174 million Chinese with $264 billion to spend on overseas shopping, according to a report from Bank of America Merrill Lynch. In comparison with the 109 million who spent $164 billion in 2014, China has been the world's largest outbound tourism market since 2012, according to data from UNWTO.

Top 10 overseas shopping destinations for Chinese travelers in 2019 were Japan, UAE(the United Arab Emirates), United Kingdom, France, Singapore, United

States, Spain, South Korea, Italy and Australia. China's luxury travelers' "love affair with all things France" was unlikely to change any time soon. More than 40% of those surveyed cited France as being in their top 10 preferred destinations to travel to. Within China, Sanya in Hainan Province, Hong Kong and Yunnan Province are the top three spots for luxury travelers to visit.

Female outbound travelers were more enthusiastic about shopping during their overseas trips, accounting for 55% of the total outbound travelers who shopped; however, the average shopping expenditure per capita by their male counterparts were 1.15 times more. More female travelers sought bargains and discounts when they traveled overseas, with 64% of the coupons on Trip.com Group's shopping channel obtained by females.

The total shopping spending by the generation born in the 1980s ranked at the top, and the generation born in 2000 started traveling and shopping abroad.

Chinese tourists' huge buying power has made them become known as "walking wallets", but some of them are often restricted on time, especially those who are part of a tour group, so anything to make the process smoother—for example, easy payment methods—will be valued. Thanks to mobile payment services such as WeChat Pay and Alipay, perhaps "walking e-wallets" would be a better nickname.

WeChat Pay's overseas service is available for Chinese tourists in 12 countries and regions, including Thailand, South Korea, Japan and Canada, Many Chinese visitors used WeChat Pay in convenience stores and duty-free shops and restaurants abroad.

Alipay is also popular with Chinese tourists overseas. With about 450 million users, Alipay is accepted by more than 80000 companies worldwide. Apart from the advantages and convenience of mobile payments, such as no need to take wallet and to wait for small change, some discount and no commission, they are not without security risks. Recently for the security reasons, Alipay has introduced new digital payment methods to users, allowing customers to process payments using a "voiceprint".

Chinese tourists are often tasked with hunting down a list of gifts for family and friends when they travel abroad, so in-store WiFi is another valuable service for shoppers, especially as it allows them to send images of the goods to recipients back home for on-the-spot approval.

Tourists usually buy a souvenir to remind them of their trip. Shopping has long been a byproduct of traveling. Recently, shopping itself has become a reason for traveling. Therefore, it's essential for a tourist professional to have the knowledge of smart shopping so that he can counsel his tourists on how to buy wisely.

# Unit 9  Tourist Shopping

## Situational Dialogue

### ➢ Dialogue 1

**Getting Information About Souvenirs**

Scene: The tour leader (A) is giving information about souvenirs to his guest, Mr. Jackson (B).

A: How do you like China, Mr. Jackson?

B: I really enjoy our stay in China. By the way, I'm planning to buy some souvenirs. Could you give me some recommendations?

A: Certainly. In China, the best souvenirs to buy are tea, silk, handicrafts, jades, paintings and calligraphies, antiques, etc. When going shopping in the local markets or department stores, you will have much more good choices.

B: Well, silk has brought fame to China. How about buying silk?

A: Good choice. Silk can be readily found in a dazzling array of colors, patterns and textures. I highly recommend it.

B: Where is the best place to buy silk in China?

A: The most distinguished silk products are found in Hangzhou, The pattern of Hangzhou silk production is derived from the nature and daily life, the flowers, pavilions, terraces and open halls, small bridge flowing water in four seasons. You always find one for yourself. All of them are pleasantly colored and soft and smooth to the touch.

B: Do we have any chance to do some silk shopping in Hangzhou?

A: Sure. Hangzhou is our last stop and we will spend half day in the famous Hangzhou silk market which sells all kinds of silk, silk clothing, silk scarves, ties.

B: Wow, I really look forward to it. Thank you very much.

A: My pleasure.

### ➢ Dialogue 2

**At a Tea Shop**

Scene: The boss (A) of a tea shop is receiving a foreign guest (B) who wants to buy some tea as gifts.

A: Can I help you?

B: Yes, I am looking for some tea for my friends. But I don't know much about it. I heard that China is the first country to plant and to drink tea. Is it true?

A: It is quite true. In traditional Chinese culture, people usually show their respect, gratitude or apologies to others by offering a cup of tea.

B: What we have in the United States is usually black tea. Is that right?

A: Yes. Black tea is popular in the West.

B: What kind of tea do Chinese like best?

A: The major four consumptions in China are green tea, oolong tea, black tea and Pu'er tea. The first three types of tea are processed using similar methods but Pu'er tea uses a totally different method. It contains a kind of fungus which is believed to be healthy. The fungus will ferment on its own after the tea is processed. This is why expensive Pu'er tea is always quite old.

B: I heard that Pu'er tea is very popular in Japan.

A: It is also popular in China. People think it can help them lose weight and control their blood pressure. Green tea is good for longevity and combating cancer. Black tea is good for keeping the stomach warm.

B: I think it's better to take some local green tea.

A: I am also a green tea drinker. Apart from the fragrance, I enjoy the green tea leaves dancing in the glass. It's very poetic.

B: That sounds great. Can I try this box of green tea please?

A: Sure. We make green tea in a glass. Look, how beautiful the picture is. Here you are. You could appreciate the tea leave dancing first, then enjoy the aroma and finally take a sip.

B: Hum, it is fragrant ... and tastes good. I really enjoy it.

A: Tea can be used as medicine and food, too.

A: Wow, I have such a lot to learn. How much is it?

A: 350 yuan a box.

B: Hmm ... It's a little overpriced. Can you give me a better deal on bulk purchases?

A: How many boxes would you like then?

B: I am planing to buy six boxes.

A: OK. I can give you a 30% discount. And that's my final offer.

B: That's reasonable. I will take them.

## ➢ Dialogue 3

### At the Gift Shop

Scene: A shop assistant (A) is receiving a guest (B) at the gift shop.

A: Can I help you find something? We've got some mugs, fridge magnets, and more ... they're right over there. Is there anything in particular you're looking for?

B: Yes, do you have something for kids?

A: How do you like this plush toy panda?

B: Wow, it is so cute. I would like two, please. Oh, I do like this pair of earring. What are they made of?

A: They are made of cloisonné which is a traditional craftsmanship only in China. They are elegant.

B: How much do they cost?

A: 380 yuan.

B: That's too much! Is there any discount?

A: If you buy two, I can give you a 20% discount. And do you like silk scarf? They are on sale.

B: Really?

A: All our scarves and hats are 40% off today and tomorrow. They are made of pure silk or wool.

B: This silk scarf doesn't have a price tag. How much is it?

A: It is 200 yuan after discount.

B: I will take it. Could you wrap it up for me? It's a present.

## IV Chinese Stories

### Shopping in China

Shopping is one of the highlights on any holiday and particularly in China where the shopping locations and options are endless. China is a fantastic destination that offers kinds of shopping opportunities, from the duty-free luxury department stores in Hong Kong to the local markets of Tibet. Whether you are looking for the latest fashion accessories or handicraft souvenirs, there is bound to be a shopping location just waiting for you to explore. China is the paradise for shoppers. As wonderful mementos and gifts, special merchandise of various kinds, including Chinese silk, tea, antiques, paintings and calligraphy, Chinese medicines, jade and pearls, handicrafts, are always available for choices.

Shopping in China is getting more convenient. For those who are staying in the country for just a few days, they may need their choice brands of daily necessities that can be found in most of the large department stores and shopping malls, which are springing up in the country. Western retail companies have established outlets in major cities in China that carry both domestic and imported goods. For those who want to shop for souvenirs to take home, they can look around, apart from large department stores and shopping malls, in some of the open markets such as the Xiushui Street and Panjiayuan Antique Market in Beijing. Unlike large department stores where the prices are fixed, these places are where you can and you must bargain. Bargaining is part of shopping on the streets and in the markets of China. Shopping in the street market is a lot of more fun, particularly if you enjoy haggling and saving money.

## What to buy

China offers a wide range of local products that are found nowhere else in the world. They include silk, embroidery works, tea, cloisonne, paper-cuts, herbal medicine, antiques, paintings and calligraphy, jade and pearls, handicrafts and more.

There are many exotic and unusual things to buy in China, which make wonderful souvenirs and gifts for relatives and friends back home. The following is a sample of the amazing range of goods available.

## Silk

China is the first country to manufacture and use silk. Chinese silk is famous all over the world for its magnificent quality, color and variety. Chinese silk has been known for its superior quality, exquisite patterns, and rich cultural connotations. Silk products from Hangzhou, Suzhou and Dandong are particularly good. Silk can be processed into clothes, handkerchiefs, scarves, pajamas, decorations, etc. The four major embroideries in China are Suzhou embroidery, Guangdong embroidery, Sichuan embroidery and Hunan embroidery. Suzhou is the best place for silk shopping with cheap price and guaranteed quality.

## Tea

As the hometown of tea, China owns a deep tea culture from ancient times. Today, China still accounts for 60% of tea plantations in the world and a great number of tea gardens scatter in more than 20 provinces throughout the country.

There are hundreds of varieties of Chinese tea. They can be classified into five categories—green tea, black tea, dark tea, scented tea, and oolong tea. Green tea is non-fermented. Its leaves and tea soup are green. Hangzhou Longjing (Dragon Well) green tea is considered the best green tea in China. Black tea is fermented. Its leaves and tea soup are red. Keemun tea is the best Chinese black tea, honored as "the queen of black tea" and is regarded as one of the three best black tea in the world with the other two produced from India and Sri Lanka respectively. Oolong tea is half-fermented. The character of this type is the leaf showing green in the center and red at the edge, it is commonly called green leaves with red edging. It keeps strong and long-lasting flavor even after drinking. It is mainly produced in Fujian, Guangdong and Taiwan, etc. Dark tea belongs to post-fermented tea. It is made by pressing steamed raw tea leaves and undergoing a period of aging in open air, from several months to many years. Pu'er tea is a fine dark tea from Yunnan province. Scented tea is one of the made-up green tea, which is made by putting fragrant flowers into tea embryos with scenting process. Any of them would make a wonderful gift for your friends.

## Wines and Spirits

China is one of the earliest countries in the world to make alcohol and the history can be traced back to prehistoric times. Alcoholic drinks, in ancient China, were regarded as sacred and were used only in sacrifices. Today, however, wines and spirits are becoming popular as accompaniments to Chinese food. In China, there is a saying that "A thousand cups of wine is not too much when bosom friends meet together." Nearly all important occasions are celebrated with alcohol. Chinese alcohols have a wide variety of kinds. The most popular Chinese liquor is made from grain, which literally means "white (clear) alcohol" or liquor. The most famous brand is Maotai which is an award winner at the Panama International Exposition in 1911, and this holds the title of the "National Liquor". Chinese rice wine or Mijiu is a traditional wine made from glutinous rice. With sweet taste, low alcoholicity, and rich nutrients, it has a wide appeal and is often used for culinary purposes as well as a beverage. The two famous representatives are the yellow wine produced in Shaoxing and Sanhua liquor produced in Guilin.

## Antiques

If you're an antique enthusiast, China is the place for you! Fascinating antique and curio shops and market stalls are to be found in most cities and country towns. Popular antiques in China range from Qing Dynasty artifacts such as jade, porcelain, snuff bottles to relics of the colonial era including old telephone, cameras, watches, radios, photo albums, books, toys, cigarette cases, desk lamps, posters and more. Care is needed, however, when buying expensive items to ensure, for example, that the item carries the official red seal of the shop and the sale documents are in order. Chinese law forbids the export of antiques dated earlier than 1795.

## Arts and Crafts

Arts and crafts products make ideal souvenirs and gifts. These include bronze ware, cloisonné, folk toys, jade, kites, lacquer wares, paper-cut, porcelain, pottery, seal, prints and scrolls, silk, embroidery and printed and dyed fabrics. Cloisonné made in Beijing, porcelain made in Jingdezhen in Jiangxi, embroidery from Suzhou, Hunan, Guangdong and Sichuan, Tang Tri-Color pottery horses and camels, and batik from Guizhou and Yunnan are all highly recommended. **Chinese knot** is an ancient folk art form in China; a simple but charming knot made of colorful silk thread that can bring good luck to its owner.

The "**Four Treasures of the Study**", namely writing brush, ink stick, paper, inkstone play an important part in Chinese culture. You may want a set for your own study or to give as a unique gift to your friends. The best writing materials are said to be Xuan paper and Hui ink stick from Anhui, Duan inkstone from Guangdong and Hu writing brush from Zhejiang.

**Accessories and Jewelry**

China is the perfect place to pick up accessories and jewelry. Most markets and tourist attractions will have shops selling everything from bracelets and necklaces to rings and jade accessories and jewelry. It is very important to remember that most trinkets picked up in tourist markets or at tourist sights will not be real silver or jade, and the quality will not be incredibly high. However, if you bargain hard it'll be worth it.

**Where to Buy**

From the roadside stall to the large-scale modern shopping mall, from the common store to a popular supermarket, China has numerous perfect places to shop that can satisfy all buyers' desires.

**Department Stores**

Shopping in China is easy and convenient, as various department stores are commonly found, especially in the high street. Various items for daily use, which are much cheaper, are often offered in the smaller and more ordinary roadside shops or boutiques. Whenever you need something, like everyday necessities, snacks or even clothes, you can immediately go there for your favorite things. Don't forget to try bargaining, you may get a special price.

**Shopping Mall**

In the busy streets of the downtown area, usually in the shopping center of a city, there are large-scale and high-class emporiums, in which not only the domestic brands but also many well-known international brands are sold. Everyday items, cosmetics, household appliances, bedding, clothes, and everything up-market that you wish for can be found easily to satisfy your every need. Bargaining is seldom acceptable, but there are often special promotions or end-of-season sales with an attractive price.

**Business Street**

Most large and distinctive Chinese cities, like Beijing, Shanghai, Xi'an, Hangzhou, Guangzhou, feature special business streets, where local products are on sale. Merchandise of the same kind is usually sold in the same street, which makes shopping easy and saves you time. The Hongqiao Market in Beijing, also known as the "Pearl Market", especially attracts female overseas tourists and mainly sells pearl jewelry, while Silver Street, where many boutiques are located, always tempt the youth by its modern fashion. You may also find various characteristic streets selling painting and calligraphy, handicraft, silk and embroidery, jade articles, crockery, furnishings, musical instruments, boutiques, even flowers, as well as grocery streets or food streets. Some of the business streets are pedestrian malls, where tourists can relax and shop at their leisure.

**Supermarket**

The western-style mode of sales operation, the supermarket, is becoming more and more popular in China for its convenience, competitive price and products, close to where people live. Everything you want for daily use can be found easily here. Many world-famous supermarket chains like Walmart, Carrefour and Metro entered the Chinese market by opening scores of branches in most of the larger cities. You have to pay what the price tag shows since bargaining is unacceptable. Make sure your bags are stored in the Locker Service before you start your shopping.

**Convenience Store**

In China, the convenience stores like 7-Eleven cannot be seen very often. In some big cities and the cities in southeast part of the country, it's easier to find convenience stores. However, groceries are in a large number. They neighbor the residential areas. The residents can buy some daily articles conveniently.

**Online Shopping**

China has a massive online retail market of 771 million digital consumers with more than $1 trillion yuan online sales in 2019. Alibaba's Taobao, an online retail market selling pretty much everything you could imagine, similar to a combination of eBay and Amazon. On Taobao, an order of multiple items will normally come in individual deliveries because the products are sourced from different sellers across China, producing huge amounts of unnecessary packaging. Shopping and discount festivals have also become more popular among retailers in recent years, such as Singles' Day (November 11), a day of discounts launched by Alibaba in 2009, which regularly surpasses the sales of Black Friday and Cyber Monday combined. Alibaba made 268.4 billion yuan in 24 hours on Singles' Day in 2019.

## V Listening

**1. Listen to the following dialogue and fill in the blanks.**

### Recommending Chinese Painting and Porcelain

A: Shop assistant    B: Guest

A: Good morning, madam. _____?

B: Yes, thank you. I'm interested in _____. Do you have any good paintings?

A: Yes, we do. _____?

B: That one with the landscape of Guilin seems good.

A: _____. There is a saying "East or west, Guilin landscape is best."

B: Mountains and rivers in Guilin are as beautiful as paintings. I can't wait to come back again.

A: I hope this painting will bring you some happy memories.

B: I hope so. How much is it?

A: _____.

B: I'll take it. By the way, one of my friends likes porcelain wares very much. _____?

A: _____? It is made in Jingdezhen, the capital of porcelain.

B: It is extremely beautiful. I am sure he will like it. _____?

A: _____ for the tea set. Can I get you anything else?

B: That's all, Thank you. Here is 1200 yuan.

A: _____. Thank you, madam. Have a nice trip.

**2. Listen to the dialogue and judge true (T) or false (F) for each statement.**

### Souvenirs

(1) Guilin's Three Treasures is too heavy for the long trip. (    )

(2) Mr. Jackson buys 5 silk fans with the picture of panda. (    )

(3) Tour guide recommends silk dress embroidered with phoenix for Mr. Jackson's daughter. (    )

(4) Mrs. Jackson buys a red dress. (    )

(5) The final price of the dress is 480 yuan. (    )

## VI Speaking

**1. Discussion:** Discuss the differences between China and Western countries when choosing gifts for friends and relatives, and manners when giving and receiving gifts with your partner. Take notes and share with others in your own words.

| Comparison between China and Western countries when giving gifts | | |
|---|---|---|
| | China | Western countries |
| Occasions for gifts | | |
| Types of gifts | | |
| Manners of giving gifts | | |
| Manners of receiving gifts | | |

**2. Role play. Work in pairs and act out the following dialogues.**

(1) Mr. Jackson will visit five destinations in China. They are Beijing, Xi'an, Guilin, Hangzhou and Shanghai. He wants to buy some gifts in each place for his daughter who is a college student. He is inquiring information from a travel agent.

(2) Jack likes Chinese paintings and calligraphy, so does his friend. He is inquiring information about paintings and calligraphy so as to buy some for his friend and himself.

(3) Sam is a foreign student studying in Guilin Tourism University. He wants to buy some local specialties for his family in the coming winter vacation. Wang is giving him advice.

## VII Writing

### Thank-you Note

**1. Writing Skills**

In writing a thank-you note, apart from expressing our gratitude, we may show our pleasure at such an invitation, a dinner, a party or a gift itself. The skills for writing a thank-you note are:

(1) Begin by expressing your gratitude for the gift/service.

(2) Mention specific details about how you plan to use a gift or what you enjoyed about an experience.

(3) Close by referencing the past and alluding to the future, such as "I hope to see you soon."

(4) Repeat your thanks. "Thank you again for the gift," makes the perfect last line.

**2. Sample**

Dear sir or madam,

Please accept my thanks for the lovely dinner yesterday. We enjoyed the evening greatly. It was most kind of you to introduce some new friends to us. We loved to meet those interesting people.

Thanks again for your warm hospitality.

Yours truly,
Kelly

**3. Writing Practice**

When you were in Shanghai last weekend, you visited your friend Jack and you had dinner together. Write a thank-you note to Jack for his hospitality.

## VIII Supplementary Reading

**Four Treasures of the Study**

Brush—Chinese brushes are made of animal hair, being soft and flexible. By controlling the pressing or raising of the brush, the calligrapher delivers a feeling of brush thickness or fineness, of feather-weight or of heavy-strength.

Ink—The process of ink grinding requires time and patience, thus, this process is able to make people stay calm and enter a state of mind suitable for calligraphy. Such practice of cultivation is a stage that must be gone through for studying and practicing calligraphy.

Paper—Paper is one of the four major Chinese inventions. Paper produced in Xuan county of Anhui province is the most famous, known as "Xuan paper"(宣纸). Papers for the use of calligraphy differ in their strength of ink absorption. Thus, the selection of paper is made according to the ideas the calligrapher has to present.

Inkstone—An inkstone is an essential for ink grinding and writing. Inkstone made from stones of the highest quality can produce ink of the best kind. Furthermore, the longer they are preserved, the higher their value is.

## Chinese calligraphy

Regarded as the most abstract and sublime form of art in Chinese culture, "Shu Fa" (calligraphy) is often thought to be most revealing of one's personality. Chinese calligraphy is the art of turning square Chinese characters into expressive images by the responsiveness of rice paper and speed and pressure of a pointed Chinese brush. By controlling the concentration of ink, the thickness and absorptivity of the paper, and the flexibility of the brush, the artist is free to produce an infinite variety of styles and forms. In the feudal period, ability in calligraphy was a major deciding factor in the selection of officials to the emperor's court. Calligraphy is dissimilar to other visual art techniques, in that all strokes of the brush are permanent and irreversible, demanding great care in the planning and a confident execution.

## Chinese Painting

Chinese painting is one of the oldest continuous artistic traditions in the world. The materials used in Chinese painting, brush and ink on paper and silk, have determined its character and development over thousands of years. Derived from calligraphy, it is essentially a linear art, employing brushwork to evoke images and feelings. Chinese paintings do not attempt to capture the actual physical appearance of a subject, but rather its essential nature or character. There are three main subjects of Chinese painting: human figures, landscapes, and birds and flowers.

## The Cheongsam

The Cheongsam or "Qi Pao" is a classic female costume, which many Westerners associated with Chinese women. It features at stand / high neck, loose chest, fitted waist, sides opening and varied sleeves (short, medium or full length) with tradition Chinese patterns. It is comfortable to wear and can fully set off the soft and elegant female figure, which gains growing popularity in the international fashion.

Qing Dynasty collapsed at early 20th century, women began to enjoy more freedom and improved their clothing for more comfort and freedom at movements.

Instead of adopting Western dress styles, they made changes to Qi Pao, cuffs narrower, lace trimmed thinner, varied collars and length, and tailored to be more fitting and revealing.

**Cloisonné**

Cloisonné is one of the famous arts and crafts of Beijing with a history of over 500 years. The charm and unique technology require rather elaborate and complicated processes: base-hammering, copper-strip inlay, soldering, enamel-filling, enamel-firing, polishing and gilding. The body is made of copper because it is easily hammered and stretched. It costs about six months or even a longer time to make a piece of it in the Beijing Enamel Factory. The work ranges a wide variety, from chopstick to vases.

## IX Check List

| Key Words | | | | |
|---|---|---|---|---|
| emporium | outlet | grocery | on sale | department store |
| souvenir | antique | handicraft | jade | local specialty |
| pottery | porcelain | embroidery | silk | Chinese calligraphy |
| cloisonné | lacquer ware | batik | pearl | gift shop |
| bargain | collection | show case | discount | shopping mall |
| paper-cut | Chinese knot | cheongsam | The four treasures of the study | |

| Useful Sentences |
|---|
| 1. Can I help you? |
| 2. Take your time, please. |
| 3. It's exceptional good in quality. |
| 4. We have a wide collection of handicrafts. |
| 5. If you are interested in folk arts, I would recommend paper-cut / batik / clay sculpture. |
| 6. What do you think of this one in Chinese traditional style? |
| 7. How do you like the style? |
| 8. The style is quite in fashion /out of date now. |
| 9. What is your favorite color? |
| 10. The color goes well with the skirt. |
| 11. Would you like to try it on? What size would you like? |
| 12. It just suits you. / This will fit better. |

Unit 9　Tourist Shopping

13. We have many types of T-shirts of the latest design in full range of sizes and colors.
14. It is both colorfast and shrink-proof.
15. If you step over to the showcase, you will find various examples.
16. Ties are on that counter/on that rack / in Aisle 3.
17. It is on sale this week.
18. There is a 20% discount if you buy two.
19. That is the final price.
20. Please keep the receipt after you buy something. You may need your receipt at the customs office.

# Unit 10
# New Trends of Tourism

**Learning Objectives**

After learning this part, you should be able to:
1. understand what smart tourism is and its major function.
2. learn to describe the application of high technologies in the tourism industry.
3. develop a pioneering spirit and a critical thinking ability.

## | Lead In

Classify the following festivals into corresponding parts.

| | | |
|---|---|---|
| Valentine's day | Mid-Autumn Day | Water-Splashing festival |
| Spring Festival | Christmas | Lantern Festival |
| Easter Day | Dragon Boat Festival | Thanksgiving Day |
| Tomb-sweeping Day | April Fool's Day | Halloween |

| Chinese Festival | Western Festival |
|---|---|
|  |  |

## Background Reading

### Smart Tourism

The new era of ICT (Information and Communications Technology) has opened a wealth of new tools for the tourism industry. As the tourism industry is one of the well-suited areas where information technology is used extensively from operational and business perspectives, it is not surprising that the idea of smart tourism destinations has developed fairly quickly.

**Smart tourism** refers to the use of technologies (e.g. Internet, mobile communication and augmented reality) to collect enormous amounts of data and to provide real-time support to all stakeholders in the destination. Smart tourism is simply the process of getting touristic services through the Internet, on any language, in any part of the world. The aim of the touristic organizations becomes to make their services accessible and easy to use.

Smart tourism is characterized by connectivity through web-based applications with location capabilities; tourists as co-producers of destination content; enhancing experiences through new technologies (augmented reality); connecting and interacting with local communities and other tourists in the destination; and improving social and environmental sustainability.

In smart tourism, technology is infrastructure that integrates hardware, software and network technologies to provide real-time data, which enables more intelligent decision-making for all stakeholders. Mobile technologies, especially the use of smart phones and their application, have a significant influence on smart tourism development.

"Smart tourism" is a brand-new proposition. It is an application of Internet of things, cloud computing, next generation communication network, high-performance information processing, intelligent data mining and other technologies in tourism experience, industrial development, administrative management and other aspects. It makes tourism physical resources and information resources highly systematic integration, deep development and activation, and serves the public, enterprises and government. Smart tourism contributes to sustainable development and responsibility of the area of tourism, replacing paper maps, dictionaries and guidebooks by electronic analogs, cutting out unnecessary usage of printed copies. This reduces the usage of paper in the hospitality services and expenses on printing and delivering these products.

Smart tourism is a new tourism form for the future. It is based on integrated communication and information technology, centered on tourists' interactive experience, guaranteed by integrated industry information management, and characterized by stimulating industrial innovation and promoting industrial structure upgrading. Smart tourism is to use mobile cloud computing, Internet and other new technologies, with the help of portable terminal Internet devices, actively perceive tourism related information, and timely arrange and adjust tourism plans. In short, it is the real-time interaction between tourists and the Internet, which makes the travel arrangement enter the era of touch.

**Major Function**

From the perspective of users, smart tourism mainly includes four basic functions: navigation, guide, tour guide and shopping guide.

**1. Start location service—navigation.**

Location Based Service (LBS) is added to travel information to let tourists know their location at any time. There are many methods to determine the location, such as GPS navigation, base station positioning, WiFi Positioning, RFID (Radio Frequency Identification) positioning, landmark positioning and so on. General smart phones have GPS navigation module. If the GPS navigation module with external Bluetooth and USB interface is used, laptop, netbook and tablet PC can have navigation function.

The traditional navigator can not be updated in time, let alone find a large number of the latest information; while the Internet has a large amount of information, but can not navigate. High-end smart phones have navigation and can also access the Internet, but the two are not combined, so it is not convenient to switch between navigation and Internet constantly.

Smart tourism integrates navigation and Internet in one interface. Maps come from the Internet, not stored on the terminal, so it is not necessary to update maps frequently. When GPS determines the location, the latest information will be actively popped up through the Internet, such as traffic congestion, traffic control, traffic accidents, traffic restrictions, parking lot and parking space conditions, and other relevant information can be found. Combining with the Internet is the future development trend of navigation industry. Through the built-in or external GPS equipment / module, with the tablet computer connected to the Internet, the mobile car can be navigated, and the location information, map information and network information can be displayed in one interface. With the change of location, all kinds of information are updated and displayed on the web page and map. It reflects the characteristics of directness, initiative, timeliness and convenience.

## 2. Preliminary understanding of the surrounding information—tour guide.

At the same time, the website and map will actively display the surrounding tourism information, including the location and general information of scenic spots, hotels, restaurants, entertainment, stations, activities (locations), friends / tour group friends, etc., such as the level and main description of the scenic spots, the star level of the hotel, the price range, the number of rooms left, and the activities (concerts, sports) location, time, price range, taste of the restaurant, per capita consumption level, discount.

You can also find the information on the non-intelligent map by dragging it on the map. The size of the surrounding area can be automatically adjusted with the size of the map window, and the walking route can be planned according to one's own interest points (such as scenic spots and the location of a friend).

## 3. Deeply understand the surrounding information—guide.

By clicking (touching) the objects of interest (scenic spots, hotels, restaurants, entertainment, stations, activities, etc.), you can get information about the location, text, pictures, videos, users' comments of the points of interest, so as to have a deep understanding of the details of the points of interest for tourists to decide whether they need them or not.

Many tourist attractions in China do not allow tour guides to explain aloud, but use digital navigation equipment, such as the Forbidden City, which requires tourists to rent such equipment. Smart tourism is like a self-help tour guide. It has more information sources than tour guides, such as text, pictures, videos and 3D virtual reality. With headphones, you can replace digital navigation equipment with mobile phone or tablet computer, and there is no need to rent such equipment.

The navigation function will also build a virtual travel module. As long as you submit the location of the starting point and destination, you can get the best route suggestions (or you can choose your own route), recommend scenic spots and hotels, and provide the main scenic spots, hotels, restaurants, entertainment, stations, activities and other information along the way. If a certain line is approved, the data can be printed out or stored in the system for calling at any time.

## 4. Waiting for enjoyment—shopping guide.

After comprehensive and in-depth online understanding and analysis, you already know what you need, so you can directly book online (room / ticket). Just feel yourself on the web.

## Ⅲ Situational Dialogue

➢ **Dialogue 1**

**Tech-savvy Traveler**

Scene: Wang Lei (A) is talking with his friend Jasmine (B) about her travel experience.

A: Hi, Jasmine, how come they call you a tech-savvy traveler?

B: I've been to roughly 100 cities in more than 20 countries. The right technology can make traveling smoother, smarter and cheaper.

A: You must have done a lot of homework before your trip. Did you take a *Lonely Planet* with you?

B: No. I travel far and wide with nothing but my mobile phone over the years. I can get everything I need on the road using various software applications, deciding where to go on holiday used to involve hours of scouring guidebooks for tips on attractions, decent hotels and how to get around in a foreign land. Now, all I need is my smart phone.

A: Really? What is the most important App you often use?

B: I first download public transportation App whenever I want to visit a new city.

A: Why is that?

B: I then book hotels based on their proximity to the subway station and maps out my travel itinerary on the public transportation network.

A: How brilliant you are!

B: I also use Apps developed by domestic travel agencies, including Tuniu and Ctrip to book train and flight tickets, and travel website Mafengwo for tips from other travelers.

A: Other traveler's experiences do help a lot.

B: Now more and more QR codes are being set on some historical buildings and exhibits in the museum, you can access to their background information with your smart phones. You can "read" the architecture or antiques. They wouldn't be just another old house or pile of rubble since you fully learn about their significance.

A: Wow. That is amazing! The tourists will have a better travel experience with this kind of digital guide service. How do you communicate with local people? You can speak a little English, right?

B: Many Apps work as interpreters and dictionaries and solve the language barrier now, such as Google Translate, Duolingo, HelloTalk, Triplingo, etc. There are even applications that can interpret the signage by capturing photos convert to conversion from audio to text.

A: Awesome! That could just be my life.

## ➤ Dialogue 2

### Flash Packer

Scene: Wang Lei (A) is talking about a new phrase with Jack(B).

A: Jack, I heard that you claimed yourself as a flash packer. It is quite a new phrase for me.

B: Well, flash packer is one who travels with the intrepid ethos of a backpacker but having added comfort, style and technology whilst still maintaining a sense of exploration and adventure.

A: Are you still traveling independently?

B: Yes. You know what a typical backpacker is, right?

A: Yes. A typical backpacker tends to do whatever they can to stretch their dollars and keep moving for as long as possible. They cut costs by choosing the cheapest accommodation option such as a backpacker hostel. They select a mode of transport that may take twice as long but is half the price. And they will favor low cost street food and bakeries over restaurants. The upside to this is it really immerses the traveler in the true culture of the place, as they spend more time "living like the locals", which generates a far more genuine travel experience.

B: As a flash packer, we want to travel to all the usual backpacker haunts and beyond, have fun and adventure, but we still have income from somewhere and will spend more money on comfort and experience. If there's a great deal to be found, that provides a little extra luxury, we're onto it.

A: You are budget-conscious, but at the same time is willing to spend a little more on comfort or to make the best use of your time.

B: Yes. We would pick a one-hour flight for $100 instead of a 12-hour chicken bus. We can't afford, and don't always want to stay in large 4-star hotels but we're happy to spend a few extra dollars a night to get an air-conditioned room with a hot shower and TV in a nice hotel or guesthouse with a pool. We'll take the occasional splurge at that 4-star hotel but we certainly won't be paying full price. We will treat ourselves to different restaurants as well as sampling the local cuisine.

A: That makes sense!

B: As for me, I would go and get long term leases or medium term leases at apartments in a place for anywhere from one to six months, and enjoy what it feels like to actually live somewhere.

A: Is that costly for staying in a place for such a long time?

B: On the contrary, it can actually save you a lot of money—a week in a hotel can cost about the same as a month in an apartment.

A: That is awesome!

B: Although the sights and everything are cool, and hanging out with tourists can be fun, I much prefer to go down to the local café, open up my laptop, talk to the people that are working there, and really get a sense for what it's like to live in a city.

A: I totally agree with you. Being a short-term vacationer is relaxing, fun, but we don't really explore the local life.

B: Exactly! You have really good friends there. One of the downsides of being a tourist is that you can never really develop friendships. And so what I found is that I go back to revisit a lot of the places that I once lived because I have lifelong friendships there.

A: That sounds exciting! But it's like a really big step, I think a lot of people would be really hesitant to do that.

B: Start by planning your trip with "I'm going to learn how to surf or I'm going to learn how to cook local food or I'm going to learn the language." You'd really enjoy a slow travel.

A: This is achievable for me. Thank you very much.

## Ⅳ Chinese Stories

### Technology and Tourism

September 27th is World Tourism Day, which has been celebrated each year by the United Nations World Tourism Organization (UNWTO) since 1980. The theme of 2018 is "Tourism and the Digital Transformation", as digital technology has greatly affected the tourism industry.

High-tech transportation services give tourists in China a more pleasant and efficient travel experience. The high-speed railway network enables tourists to travel to far away places for less money and time. And the facial recognition systems used at an increasing number of railway stations and airports help speed up security screening and ticket checks for travelers.

Technologies such as virtual reality, augmented reality, and artificial intelligence enable tourists to enjoy entertaining and interactive visual experiences. With ever-improving headsets, smart phones and WiFi connections, technologies have changed the way we travel, bringing the 360-degree experience of museums, theme parks and historical sites to our homes. In 2019, NASA provided a VR experience of Mars, allowing people to "walk" its surface with just a headset. Paris' famous museums, meanwhile, provided more applications with AR technology. This gives visitors more context and information about exhibits. With that, visitors can view a sea cow growing flesh before their eyes. A growing number of China's tourist attractions, including theme parks, museums, and even zoos are applying those technologies to attract visitors.

The Palace Museum is a leader in the use of these technologies. The famous museum, popularly known as the Forbidden City, put on a digital exhibition in October 2017 to make its silent historical relics come alive. By wearing a VR helmet in a moving seat, visitors felt as if they were walking through the famous landmark during ancient times. They were even able to talk with a virtual senior minister with the help of artificial intelligence. In this way, visitors enjoyed a truly immersive experience that combined vision, sound, and movement. The Palace Museum also opened a digital gallery to show images of items, which are too old and fragile to put on public display.

In April 2018, an intelligent robot tour guide was put to use in a scenic area in Changsha, Hunan Province. The robot named Yoyo showed tourists around and gave a brief introduction for the scenic spot. It could sing and dance to amuse visitors. And thanks to voice recognition software, it could even answer questions from tourists.

The latest technology, including artificial intelligence and intelligent robots, has also been used in some hotels. China's e-commerce giant Alibaba Group has unveiled its first "future hotel", also known as "FlyZoo Hotel" in Hangzhou, China in 2018. The hotel's operation relies on smart interactive technologies, particularly facial recognition.

It all starts with the FlyZoo mobile App. From there, travelers can book their stays, choose the floor they want and even the direction their room faces. FlyZoo features a range of artificial intelligence-powered services to create a convenient, seamless experience for guests. For example, they can choose to use facial recognition—rather than keys and key cards—to access the hotel. That means everything from using the elevator to entering their room is as easy as smiling for the camera. FlyZoo uses the photos taken at check-in to verify that the users are staying at the hotel. A 1-meter high robot serves as a receptionist, remembering guests by using facial recognition technology. For foreign passport holders, check-in requires just a few simple steps at a kiosk with help from hotel staff. But Chinese travelers can check in via the App and go straight to their room. And the elevator can also identify the customer's room by identifying the customer's identity, and then stop at the corresponding floor.

Each room is equipped with a Tmall Genie smart assistant, which helps guests adjust the temperature, lights, curtains and the TV, plays music and even answers simple questions—such as "What is the WiFi password?"—all with a simple voice command. If they want fresh water for the room, or new pillows, Tmall Genie can handle that as well, and they'll be delivered by an Alibaba-made robot. When it's time to check out, there are no lines and no hassle. Guests just pack and go. If they have to leave before the standard checkout time, they can choose to tell the hotel in advance by using the App. Their rooms will automatically be released after checkout.

FlyZoo still employs humans—to run housekeeping. Robots can be found everywhere in the hotel, and they guide guests by providing recorded voice messages and accompanying them during their stay. Guests can also control indoor temperatures, lighting intensity, and household appliances through their voices. FlyZoo Hotel also has seven themed rooms, each of which is able to create a better living experience for its guests.

To sum up, technologies have great impact on China's tourism. The future of travel is technology-based, so tourism jobs will require both technical and advanced skills used to effectively manage smart operations. The greatest impact of digital transformation on tourism may be the effect on the sector's workforce, which directly and indirectly represents 1 in every 10 jobs worldwide.

## Ⅴ Listening

**1. Listen to the dialogue and fill in the blanks.**

### Responsible Tourism

A: Nowadays, many people try to live in a way _____
_____.

B: How could they achieve this target?

A: They _____, take public transport to get to work, and _____.

B: That's great! We _____ with us.

A: This is why alternative forms of tourism are becoming popular in the world. There are lots of names for these new forms of tourism: _____, nature tourism, _____, educational tourism and more.

B: Is there any common standards for these tourism?

A: Although everyone may have a different definition, most people agree that these new forms of tourism should do the following. First, they should _____ Second, they should _____. Third, they should _____. And finally, they should provide an experience that tourists want to pay for.

B: As a tourist, we should _____.

Unit 10　New Trends of Tourism

A: That's true. Besides, it should deliver "_____
_____"—with the emphasis firstly on creating better places for local people, and secondly for tourists.

B: I hope that everyone can _____ in our daily life.

A: Yes. Start with ourselves.

**2. Listen to the dialogue and judge true (T) or false (F) for each statement.**

Solo Travel

(1) Christine enjoys eating alone in the cafeteria. (　　)

(2) People usually think that eating alone means you dislike socializing with others. (　　)

(3) The survey shows that average adult eat five meals alone each week. (　　)

(4) Solo travel has become popular especially among young people recently. (　　)

(5) Traveling alone in a foreign country can develop your self-confidence and meet interesting people. (　　)

(6) You can change your mind as often as you want when you are traveling alone. (　　)

扫码
听听力

## Ⅵ Speaking

1. Discussion: Here are some important Apps in China's tourism industry. Discuss with your neighbor and find out the services they offer and their pros and cons.

| Comparison among tourism Apps | | |
|---|---|---|
| | Services | Pros and cons |
| Ctrip | | |
| Mafengwo | | |
| Qyer | | |
| TripAdvisor | | |
| Yelp | | |

**2. Role play: Work in pairs and act out the following dialogues.**

(1) Two friends are talking about the social medias that they use to get travel information.

(2) Wang is introducing the necessary Apps a foreigner needs when traveling in China to Rick, his foreign friend from the United States.

(3) Jack is talking about the VR experience he had in a museum with his friend.

## Ⅶ Writing

### Farewell Speech

**1. Writing Skills**

A complete farewell speech should contain following parts:

(1) Express your reluctance to the guests.

(2) Thanks to the guests for their cooperation and support.

(3) Hopes guests enjoy their trip home.

(4) Welcome guests to China again.

**2. Sample**

Ladies and Gentlemen,

The time has gone by quickly and your trip to China is drawing to a close. It's a pity that you cannot stay in our country any longer. Then allow me to take this opportunity to say goodbye to you.

I would like to tell you that it is a great pleasure for me to spend the last few days as your guide. I have had the opportunity to meet and get to know you, and we have spent a great deal of time together. I hope you have enjoyed these few days as much as I have. We have tried to make your stay here in China as pleasant and enjoyable as possible. We sincerely hope that you have enjoyed being here and that one day in the future you will return to visit us again. If there is anything we can do to make this possible, please feel free to call us.

I wish to thank you all for the cooperation and support you have given us in the past several days. You have kept good time on all occasions, which made things a lot easier for me. You have been very attentive when we had anything to tell you. I'd like to add that you are the best group we've ever been with.

Several days ago, we met as strangers; today, we say goodbye to each other as friends. A Chinese saying goes, "A good friend from afar brings a distant land closer." I hope you'll take back happy memories of your trip to China and you are welcome to come back sometime in the future.

As you have probably observed, China is developing very quickly. When and if you come back in the future, our country may have changed beyond recognition. Meanwhile, I will continue my humble job as a tour guide. I wish to see you again in the future and to be your guide.

Once again, thank you for your cooperation and support.

Goodbye!

### 3. Writing Practice

If you are a tour guide, try to write a farewell speech for the tourists that going to leave Guilin.

## VIII Supplementary Reading

### Ecotourism

Ecotourism is defined as "responsible travel to natural areas that preserves the environment and improves the welfare of the local people" by the International Ecotourism Society. It is different from traditional tourism because it allows the traveler to become educated about the areas—both in terms of the physical landscape and cultural characteristics, and often provides funds for conservation and benefits the economic development of places that are frequently impoverished. Ecotourism and other forms of sustainable travel have their origins with the environmental movement of the 1970s. Ecotourism itself did not become prevalent as a travel concept until the late 1980s. During that time, increasing environmental awareness and a desire to travel to natural locations as opposed to built up tourist locations made ecotourism desirable.

To be considered ecotourism, a trip must meet the following principles set forth by the International Ecotourism Society: a. Minimize the impact of visiting the location (i.e. the use of roads); b. Build respect and awareness for the environment and cultural practices; c. Ensure that the tourism provides positive experiences for both the visitors and the hosts; d. Provide direct financial aid for conservation; e. Provide financial aid, empowerment and other benefits for local people; f. Raise the traveler's awareness of the host country's political, environmental and social climate.

### Timeshare

A timeshare is a shared ownership model of vacation real estate in which multiple purchasers own allotments of usage, typically in one-week increments, in the same property. The timeshare model can be applied to many different types of properties, such as vacation resorts, condominiums, apartments, and campgrounds.

With a timeshare, you own an allotted amount of "time" during which you have access to your resort accommodations, and the amount you pay for ownership and maintenance is proportionally less. Timesharing works for many travelers, because you get the benefits of a high-end vacation home without the high cost of expenses and upkeep. Most timeshare ownership programs now also offer the option to exchange your timeshare for a vacation at a different resort in a different location—so you are not tied down to the same spot year after year. Compared to traditional hotel rooms, vacation timeshares are far more deluxe and can range in size from studio units to suites with three or more bedrooms that can often sleep ten or more guests.

Timeshare offers additional conveniences and comforts not available to travelers who stay exclusively in hotels. In addition to the in-suite amenities, timeshare resorts also provide an extensive range of on-site activities and amenities. Many resorts offer championship golf courses, ski mountain access, equestrian centers, water complexes, world-class spas and even five-star restaurants.

## WeChat

WeChat is the most popular messaging service in China, and is great if you're meeting people in China and want to stay in touch. Even in cases where you, for example, meet a lovely taxi driver and want to keep him in touch in case you need him to drive you around the next day, WeChat is the best way to do this.

You can send text and voice messages, and call people for free if you're both connected to either WiFi, 4G or 5G. It can also be used to pay for things by QR code.

## QQ

QQ is a popular Chinese communication App that allows you to instant message contacts, video chat, and meet new friends easily. It was one of the most popular Apps before WeChat came to the market. Once WeChat became available, **QQ** was not used as frequently as before, because WeChat has more user-friendly features for social interaction. Now **QQ** remains an important App for schools for communication between teachers and parents. It provides many important functions relating to study and family work.

## Alipay

Alipay is a commonly used third-party online payment solution in China. Launched in 2004, it provides an easy, safe and secure way for millions of individuals and businesses to make and receive payments on the Internet. Alipay has its origins in a service devised for Taobao, an online platform run by Alibaba where small businesses sell directly to Chinese consumers. Customers were reluctant to pay for goods before they had received them. So buyers would send their orders by fax to Alipay to hold their money in escrow and release it when delivery was confirmed. In

2008 this system was transformed into mobile "wallets" in which the money is held. It is currently the largest online payment solution provider in China now. Alipay has more than 1 billion registered accounts as of 2019. It can be used both in person at a vast majority of establishments (any place that shows its blue and orange logo, labeled "Alipay" or in Chinese below), as well as online, or simply to send money to friends.

**VR**

Virtual Reality has been a part of science fiction for some time but not anymore. This technology is fast changing the way we look at many things. Once connected to a computer or mobile device, a VR headset gives users a complete 3D experience, making them feel as if they are walking around inside a virtual world.

The best VR travel Apps now available can immerse you completely into a place or a specific city, museum, park, resort or hotel before you take the plunge. For this, all you need is a VR headset, like the Google Cardboard or Gear VR and a VR supported smart phone. VR technology can greatly ease the decision making process. With VR anyone can tour your city, island or country from anywhere. Virtual tours are an effective way to plan activities for the trip. VR rolls out exotic locations and activities in a "try before buy" format. And this helps you to shake off confusion about any tourist spots or schedules.

## IX Check List

| Key Words | | | | |
|---|---|---|---|---|
| technology | interactive | recognition | digital | Virtual Reality |
| immersive | mobile | navigation | haunt | farewell speech |
| artificial | intelligence | facial | helmet | Augmented Reality |
| Useful Sentences | | | | |

1. How time flies!
2. Your current visit to Guilin is drawing to a close.
3. It is time for us to say goodbye to each other.
4. Please get your air ticket, group visa and boarding pass ready.

5. I hope you all have enjoyed your stay.
6. We thank you for your patience and friendliness.
7. I wish to thank you all for the cooperation and support.
8. I also appreciate you for your cooperation and understanding.
9. We look forward to seeing you again.
10. Wish you a pleasant trip to your next destination.
11. I would like to welcome you back.
12. Bon voyage!

# 参考文献
References

[1] 马飞,司爱侠. 旅游专业英语实用教程[M]. (2版). 北京:清华大学出版社,2016.
[2] 赵海湖,王宁. 旅游英语[M]. 北京:清华大学出版社,2020.
[3] Huimin Gu, Chris Ryan, Larry Yu. The changing structure of the Chinese hotel industry:1980—2012[J]. Tourism Management Perspectives,2012(4).
[4] 约翰·弗莱彻,艾伦·法伊奥,戴维·吉尔伯特,等. 旅游学:理论与案例[M]. (5版). 沈阳:东北财经大学出版社,2014.
[5] Loykie Lomine,James Edmunds. 旅游学要义[M]. 李力,译. 广州:广东旅游出版社,2017.
[6] 吴晓群. 旅游英语[M]. 上海:上海交通大学出版社,2019.
[7] 教育部《旅游英语》编写组. 旅游英语[M]. 北京:高等教育出版社,2017.
[8] 段开成. 旅游管理专业英语[M]. 北京:高等教育出版社,2006.
[9] Goeldner C R, Ritchie JRB. Tourism:Principles, Practices, Philosophies[M]. John Wiley & Sons, Inc. ,2011.

# 教学支持说明

为了改善教学效果,提高教材的使用效率,满足高校授课教师的教学需求,本套教材备有与纸质教材配套的教学课件(PPT)和拓展资源(案例库、习题库等)。

为保证本教学课件及相关教学资料仅为教材使用者所得,我们将向使用本套教材的高校授课教师免费赠送教学课件或相关教学资料,烦请授课教师通过电话、邮件或加入旅游专家俱乐部QQ群等方式与我们联系,获取"电子资源申请表"文档,准确填写后反给我们,我们的联系方式如下:

地址:湖北省武汉市东湖新技术开发区华工科技园华工园六路

邮编:430223

电话:027-81321911

传真:027-81321917

E-mail:lyzjjlb@163.com

旅游专家俱乐部QQ群号:758712998

旅游专家俱乐部QQ群二维码:

# 电子资源申请表

填表时间：_____年___月___日

1. 以下内容请教师按实际情况填写，★为必填项。
2. 根据个人情况如实填写，可以酌情调整相关内容提交。

| ★姓名 | | ★性别 | □男 □女 | 出生年月 | | ★职务 | |
|---|---|---|---|---|---|---|---|
| | | | | | | ★职称 | □教授 □副教授 □讲师 □助教 |

| ★学校 | | ★院/系 | |
|---|---|---|---|
| ★教研室 | | ★专业 | |
| ★办公电话 | | 家庭电话 | | ★移动电话 | |
| ★E-mail | | ★QQ号/微信号 | |
| ★联系地址 | | ★邮编 | |

| ★现在主授课程情况 | 学生人数 | 教材所属出版社 | 教材满意度 |
|---|---|---|---|
| 课程一 | | | □满意 □一般 □不满意 |
| 课程二 | | | □满意 □一般 □不满意 |
| 课程三 | | | □满意 □一般 □不满意 |
| 其他 | | | □满意 □一般 □不满意 |

| 教材出版信息 | | | | | |
|---|---|---|---|---|---|
| 方向一 | □准备写 | □写作中 | □已成稿 | □已出版待修订 | □有讲义 |
| 方向二 | □准备写 | □写作中 | □已成稿 | □已出版待修订 | □有讲义 |
| 方向三 | □准备写 | □写作中 | □已成稿 | □已出版待修订 | □有讲义 |

请教师认真填写下列表格内容，提供申请教材配套课件的相关信息，我社将根据每位教师填表信息的完整性、授课情况与申请课件的相关性，以及教材使用的情况赠送教材的配套课件及相关教学资源。

| ISBN（书号） | 书名 | 作者 | 申请课件简要说明 | 学生人数（如选作教材） |
|---|---|---|---|---|
| | | | □教学 □参考 | |
| | | | □教学 □参考 | |

★您对与课件配套的纸质教材的意见和建议有哪些，希望我们提供哪些配套教学资源：